PENGUIN BOOKS

SIX MINUTES OF TERROR

Nazia Sayed has been a crime reporter for over a decade, with experience in television and print journalism. Currently working as a special correspondent with *Mumbai Mirror*, Nazia is credited with breaking several stories, which includes her exposé on the Mumbai mafia and the ISIS network in the country. Her crime stories have won her accolades in the Indian as well as international press.

Sharmeen Hakim is a legal correspondent with *Mumbai Mirror*, known for her impeccable court reporting. Apart from the Malegaon blasts and the 'Mumbai triple blasts', she covered the 7/11 trial for three years until it concluded last year. Only twenty-four, Sharmeen is widely respected in the fraternity for being one of the most thorough court journalists in the city, and for her strong grasp of the law.

S. HUSSAIN ZAIDI PRESENTS

SIX MINUTES OF
TERROR

The Untold Story of the
7/11 Mumbai Train Blasts

NAZIA SAYED and **SHARMEEN HAKIM**

**BLUE
SALT**

PENGUIN BOOKS

An imprint of Penguin Random House

PENGUIN BOOKS

USA | Canada | UK | Ireland | Australia
New Zealand | India | South Africa | China | Singapore

Penguin Books is part of the Penguin Random House group of companies
whose addresses can be found at global.penguinrandomhouse.com

Published by Penguin Random House India Pvt. Ltd
4th Floor, Capital Tower 1, MG Road,
Gurugram 122 002, Haryana, India

First published in Penguin Books by Penguin Random House India and
Blue Salt 2016

10 9 8 7 6 5 4 3 2

The views and opinions expressed in this book are the authors' own and the
facts are as reported by them which have been verified to the extent possible,
and the publishers are not in any way liable for the same.

ISBN 9780143426547

Typeset in Adobe Jenson Pro by Manipal Digital Systems, Manipal
Printed at Repro India Limited

www.penguin.co.in

This is a legitimate digitally printed version of the book and therefore might not
have certain extra finishing on the cover.

For my inspiration, Iffat Barodawala,
and my parents, Husain Abdul Gafoor Sayed and Zubeda Sayed

Contents

Terror on Mumbai Trains

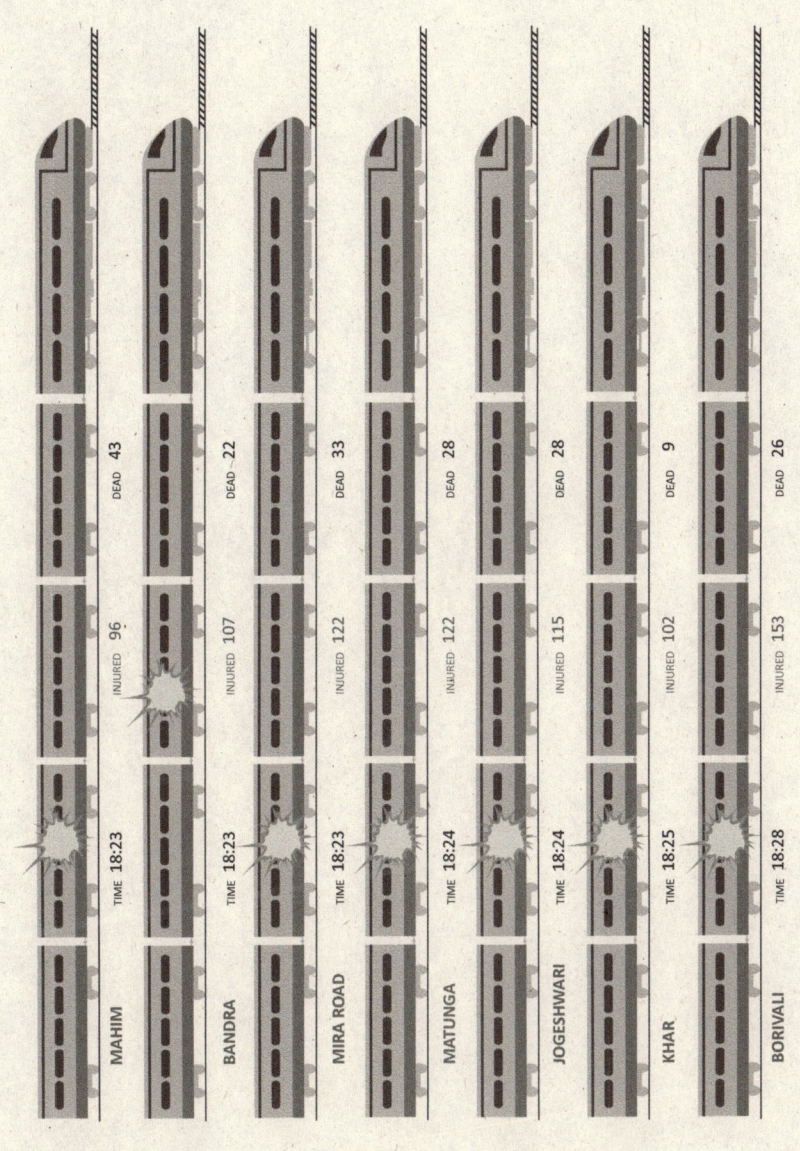

MAHIM   TIME **18:23**   INJURED **96**   DEAD **43**

BANDRA   TIME **18:23**   INJURED **107**   DEAD **22**

MIRA ROAD   TIME **18:23**   INJURED **122**   DEAD **33**

MATUNGA   TIME **18:24**   INJURED **122**   DEAD **28**

JOGESHWARI   TIME **18:24**   INJURED **115**   DEAD **28**

KHAR   TIME **18:25**   INJURED **102**   DEAD **9**

BORIVALI   TIME **18:28**   INJURED **153**   DEAD **26**

Timeline of the Blasts

28 September 2001

Just twenty days after the 9/11 attacks on the World Trade Center in New York, the Students Islamic Movement in India (SIMI) is banned for fuelling unrest across the country.

11 July 2006

Bombs laden with Research Department Explosive (RDX) destroy seven first-class compartments of seven different trains on the Western Line of the Mumbai local train network. All the blasts occur within a span of six minutes, killing 189 people and injuring 829 others.

20 July 2006

The Anti-Terrorism Squad (ATS) has its first breakthrough in the case with the arrest of Kamal Ansari in Bihar. For the first time since its inception in 2005, investigators from the agency take a flight to make an arrest. The half kilogram of RDX seized from his house is brought back to Mumbai in a train.

26 August 2006

Assistant Commissioner of Police Vinod Bhat, investigating the 7/11 train blasts, commits suicide. He is run over by a train. The reason behind his death remains a mystery.

8 September 2006

Four bombs explode in Malegaon just after Friday namaz on the holy day of Shab-e-Baraat. Three bombs explode in the Bada Kabristan compound and one at Mushawarat Chowk, 500 metres away. Thirty-one people are killed and 312 injured.

29 September 2006

After a long gap, the ATS arrests four more people in the 7/11 serial train blasts case. They are Abdul Wahideen Mohammad Shaikh, his brother-in-law Sajid Marghoob Ansari, Mohammed Ali Alam Shaikh and Mohammed Majid Shafi from Kolkata.

30 September 2006

In a memorable press conference, A.N. Roy, commissioner of police, Mumbai, Parvinder Singh Pasricha, the director general of police, and K.P. Raghuvanshi, chief of the ATS, announce that they have cracked the 7/11 train blasts case with the arrest of twelve men (Asif Bashir Khan is arrested later). They announce that the bombs were placed in pressure cookers and assembled in four different parts of the city. They declare that the Lashkar-e-Taiba (LeT) was responsible for the blasts, with the support of SIMI members. In the following days, confessions of eleven of the thirteen accused are recorded after the stringent Maharashtra Control of Organised Crime Act (MCOCA) is invoked.

30 November 2006

The ATS files a 10,667-page charge sheet accusing the thirteen arrested Indians and fifteen absconding Pakistanis of the blasts. All the accused retract their confessions. However, in terms of details, the charge sheet is slightly different from the September press conference. For instance, in the press conference, the police had declared that pressure cookers were used to store the bombs, which was replaced by the words 'household utensils' in the charge sheet. It was alleged that all the bombs were assembled in a shanty in Govandi and not in different places.

29 February 2008

The Supreme Court of India stays the trial in the 7/11 train blasts case, the Aurangabad arms haul case and the 2006 Malegaon blasts case, after one accused from all three cases moves the court, through lawyer Shahid Azmi. They challenge the constitutional validity of a clause in the MCOCA, which refers to their crimes as 'insurgency'.

24 September 2008

The Mumbai Crime Branch arrests five Indian Mujahideen (IM) operatives, including Sadiq Israr Shaikh. According to their probe, the IM confessed to its involvement in all the terror attacks in the country from 2005–08. This is a huge jolt for the ATS, which has already put a completely different set of accused to trial in the 7/11 case.

26 November 2008

In the midst of this controversy, ATS chief Hemant Karkare is killed in an LeT-led terror strike on the Taj Mahal Palace hotel, Trident Hotel and Chhatrapati Shivaji Terminus (CST) railway station. Karkare had become ATS chief only that year and was responsible for busting the saffron terror module.

20 February 2009

After almost five months of back and forth, the ATS finally approaches the special court for Sadiq's custody. Almost immediately, the media is banned from reporting on the investigation into the 7/11 case.

11 May 2009

The ATS says it has found no evidence against Sadiq. He is subsequently discharged by the court.

11 February 2010

Shahid Azmi, representing some of the accused, is shot dead in his Kurla office by four unidentified men.

23 April 2010

The Supreme Court upholds the validity of the MCOCA section dealing with insurgency, thus dismissing the petition filed by the accused. The stay on all three trials is automatically lifted, paving the way for the trials to begin.

30 August 2013

Yasin Bhatkal, co-founder of the IM, is arrested near the Indo-Nepal border. Yasin claims that the 2006 bombings were the handiwork of the Indian Mujahideen and were in retaliation for the 2002 Godhra riots, raising questions about the arrests of the thirteen men accused by the ATS.

19 August 2014

After the defence and the prosecution complete their final arguments in the case, Special Judge Y.D. Shinde reserves his verdict.

11 September 2015

In an 1839-page order, Judge Shinde holds twelve men guilty and acquits only Abdul Wahid Shaikh.

30 September 2015

The five planters are sentenced to death, while the remaining are sentenced to life imprisonment.

Glossary of Legal Terms

Charge sheet: A detailed report prepared by the police on the crime, based on which a case against the accused progresses in a court.

Vakalatnama: A document authorizing a lawyer to represent a person before a court.

Panchnama: A document detailing how a particular action by an investigating agency is carried out. For instance, papers related to an arrest, inquest, search and seizure, etc.; an investigation of a crime scene relating to the seizure of incriminating articles.

Panch: An independent person (i.e. not a part of the investigating machinery) who is witness to any of the actions above.

Framing of charges: Sections under which an accused is put to trial based on the role played by him/her.

Prosecution: An advocate or a team of lawyers representing the investigating agency.

Judicial custody: When a convict is arrested, he is interrogated by the police in their lock-up, known as police custody. Once this period of interrogation is complete, the accused is kept in a prison, along with several other prisoners undergoing trial. The latter is known as judicial custody.

Amicus curiae: Loosely called 'friend of the court', an amicus curiae is an advocate appointed by the court to assist itself (the court), generally keeping a particular purpose or case in mind.

Statement under section 164 of the Criminal Procedure Code: A statement recorded by a judicial magistrate. It could be anyone—a victim, witness or accused. This statement has greater value as evidence compared to a statement recorded by a police officer because it is believed that the magistrate is unbiased.

Deposition/testimony: The process where a witness stands in the box during a trial before a court and answers the questions put to him/her. The questions could be put forward by a prosecutor, defence or the court/judge.

Roznama: Official recordings (document) by a judge about the happenings related to a particular case in the court on a given day.

Confessional statement: While in common parlance a confession is an admission of guilt, there are several rules that have to be followed while recording a confessional statement. Under the Maharashtra Control of Organised Crime Act, an officer, not below the rank of superintendent of police, is authorized to record the statement. It is supposed to be out of the accused's free will and not under pressure. In fact, to ensure this, he has to be taken to a chief metropolitan magistrate, whose job is to ascertain that the person has made the confession voluntarily. A confession is accepted in court only when all these rules are followed.

Profiles of the Accused

Convicted

Kamal Ansari (42): Death Sentence

Kamal was the first person to be arrested in the case. He hails from Basupatti, a tiny village in Bihar, close to the India–Nepal border. A father of five, Kamal and his family lived in abject poverty. He did odd jobs—he worked as a vegetable vendor, a driver and a tailor. He was sent to Pakistan by LeT operative Hafiz Zuber, a wanted accused in the case, on the pretext of collecting donations for madrasas. There, Kamal was given arms training and underwent rigorous indoctrination. He was arrested with a weapon in Delhi a few years after his return. He has been convicted of planting the bomb that went off near Matunga, as well as for aiding the entry of two Pakistanis into the country through the Nepal border. His family is so poor that they could not afford to travel to Mumbai to call on him in prison or at the court.

Dr Tanveer Ansari (42): Life Imprisonment

At the time of his arrest, Tanveer was working as a medical registrar at M.H. Saboo Siddique Maternity and General

Hospital, close to his home in Nagpada in south Mumbai. He was arrested in 2001, along with Ehtesham Siddiqui, when the Students Islamic Movement of India (SIMI) was banned. He was once the president of SIMI's local unit, but was later removed from that post. A fitness freak, Tanveer has been convicted of participating in conspiracy meetings and undergoing training in Pakistan, where he learnt to use AK-47 rifles and pistols, and how to make bombs and detonators.

Faisal Atta-ur Rahman Shaikh (42): Death Sentence

Born in Mira Road, Faisal Atta-ur Rahman Shaikh is the oldest of three brothers, with an elder sister. His family shifted to Pune from Mira Road a few years after he dropped out of college. In Pune's Mominpura area, he started visiting the local Mecca mosque regularly. He underwent training in Pakistan and was deported from Saudi Arabia in 2004. Faisal was considered the western-India commander of the LeT and, therefore, the prime executor of the attack from India. All the brothers have been accused of being involved in the train blasts. However, Rahil, younger to Faisal, is still absconding. It is believed he is working as a software engineer in Birmingham in the United Kingdom. Faisal has been convicted of organizing conspiracy meetings, possessing huge amounts of foreign currency and planting the bomb that went off at Jogeshwari.

Ehtesham Siddiqui (35): Death Sentence

Ehtesham dropped out of his engineering course after he was arrested for being a member of the SIMI in 2001. Originally from Azamgarh, he started publishing books in Mira Road, where he lived alone. Once the head of SIMI's Mira Road unit, he went all the way up to Nepal to scout for locations for training camps. In 2006, he became the general secretary of SIMI in Maharashtra. Ehtesham has been convicted for planting the bomb that went off in Mira Road and participating in conspiracy meetings.

Mohammed Majid Shafi (38): Life Imprisonment

A native of Kolkata, Majid dropped out of school while he was in class nine to join his brothers in the family business. The family owns two shoe shops in the city. Majid has seven brothers and four sisters—all residing in the same bungalow. Majid, like Kamal, had no connection with the SIMI, and was influenced by his cousin, an LeT operative. He was convicted of facilitating the entry and exit of six Pakistanis through the Bangladesh border for the blasts.

Mohammed Ali Alam Shaikh (46): Life Imprisonment

A salesman at the time of his arrest, Mohammed Ali lived with his two brothers and their families in a shanty in Govandi. A former SIMI member, Mohammed Ali met Faisal while selling beads (*tilasmi moti*) at M.H. Saboo Siddique Hospital. He has been convicted for allowing the Pakistanis to make the bombs in his shanty in Govandi and for attending several conspiracy meetings. He was later named an accused in the 2006 Malegaon blasts case.

Sajid Marghoob Ansari (39): Life Imprisonment

Sajid lived with his family—parents, two brothers and five sisters—in Mira Road. Sajid's siblings are well educated—

his sisters are professors and one of his brothers is a doctor, while the other one is an engineer. Sajid completed a diploma in industrial electronic engineering from M.H. Saboo Siddique Polytechnic College and went on to do a six-month course in computer hardware. Much later, he also learnt to repair mobile phones and slowly graduated to repairing computers. He was first arrested in 2001 for distributing SIMI pamphlets after a Quran-burning incident. He headed SIMI's Mira Road unit in 2006. Sajid was convicted for helping two Pakistanis make the bombs used in the attacks.

Muzzammil Atta-ur Rahman Shaikh (32): Life Imprisonment

Muzzammil is Faisal's youngest brother. Just a month before his arrest, Muzzammil had joined Datacore Technologies in Bangalore. While he claims to have graduated from Bhartiya Shiksha Parishad, a case was registered against him for allegedly forging his educational certificates. In 2004, like some of the other accused, Muzzammil also travelled on a Ziyarat visa to Iran and then to Pakistan for arms training. He was convicted of attending conspiracy meetings.

Suhail Mehmood Shaikh (48): Life Imprisonment

A resident of Pune, Suhail joined his family's tiffin-service business soon after he failed his board examination. Four years later, he became a full-time spiritual healer. His first brush with the law was when he was arrested for burning the American flag, three years after the Babri Masjid demolition. Faisal and Suhail, who went to the same mosque, would often meet to discuss the 'unjust' ban on SIMI. Faisal offered Suhail financial aid in return for help to plan the blasts.

Suhail trained in Pakistan in 2002. He has been convicted of attending conspiracy meetings and surveying the targets along with Faisal.

Zameer Latifur Rehman Shaikh (42): Life Imprisonment

Zameer's family owns a key shop on the footpath near Bombay Central railway station and a taxi. Zameer met Tanveer when the latter treated Zameer's wife for tuberculosis in 1999. Soon, he gravitated towards SIMI and its ideology. In 2005, Zameer went for training to Pakistan that same year, allegedly in a bid to avenge the atrocities meted out against Muslims across the world. He was convicted of surveying trains for the blasts, along with Faisal and Suhail.

Naved Hussain Khan (35): Death Sentence

A commerce graduate, Naved was working as a floor manager in RSR Sales Services Pvt. Ltd before his arrest in Secunderabad. Faisal and Naved were extremely close; they would often visit clubs together. Naved was neither a part of SIMI nor was he an extremist like most of the other convicts. He has been held guilty of planting the bomb that went off near Khar.

Asif Bashir Khan (44): Death Sentence

A civil engineer from Jalgaon in Maharashtra, Asif is the sharpest of all the convicts. He was the last one to be arrested in the case. Asif held an important position in the SIMI leadership and was wanted in several cases before the train blasts. He was convicted of being one of the key conspirators of the attacks and planting the bomb that went off at Borivali.

Acquitted

Abdul Wahid Din Mohammad Shaikh (39)

An assistant teacher with Anjuman-i-Islam A.S.S. School near Grant Road in south Mumbai, Abdul Wahid's kids were only toddlers at the time of his arrest. He was a member of SIMI and had one case registered against him soon after the organization's ban in 2001. Accused of harbouring Pakistanis involved in the blasts, Shaikh is the only one to have been acquitted in the case.

Prologue

'Laws are like cobwebs, which may catch small flies, but let wasps and hornets break through'

—Jonathan Swift

Sessions Court, room no. 57
September 2015

For two days straight, only one thought had raced through Yug Mohit Chaudhry's mind. The 6-foot-tall human rights lawyer was defending seven of the thirteen men accused in the 7/11 Mumbai train blasts case. Twelve of the accused were close to the gallows. Chaudhry had only one objective—to save these men from death. Did he actually have the audacity to believe they deserved better? Especially when the courts had already pronounced them guilty and the nation at large was waiting with bated breath for 'justice'.

He wasn't being impudent; he just considered capital punishment the highest form of barbarism in a civil society. No one deserved it.

Needless to say, while Chaudhry's stand had made him a messiah to some, he was a villain in the eyes of many, many more. After all, the convicts he was defending had been pronounced guilty of systematically carrying out seven high-intensity bomb blasts in Mumbai's local trains on 11 July 2006. The blasts ripped apart the city's lifeline, taking 189 innocent lives and leaving 829 others severely injured.

Chaudhry understood fully well that his stand wasn't going to be too popular. And he seemed to be at peace with it—something that was evident from his unfazed demeanour each time he walked through the media-infested entrance of the Venetian Gothic-style court building in south Mumbai—all the staring and murmuring notwithstanding.

In stark contrast to the pulsating energy outside the majestic building, the room in the special court under the stringent Maharashtra Control of Organised Crime Act (MCOCA), destined to seal the fate of these twelve men, exuded a sense of gloom. Partly because of its matchbox size, entry was restricted to fifty people by Special Judge Yatin D. Shinde who also often got claustrophobic.

All the buzz in the room came to a complete standstill when Chaudhry's sharp voice called the men he defended nothing more than 'delivery boys'.

He declared that the man running the show was Azam Cheema, an elusive figure known to be an operative of Pakistan's Inter-Services Intelligence (ISI) and commander of the terror outfit Lashkar-e-Taiba (LeT). Calling him the architect of the crime, Chaudhry's argument was simple: he used the 1993 bomb blast verdict as a precedent.

Back then, the Supreme Court had made a landmark distinction between the 'archers' and the 'arrows'. In other words, the planners and the executors. Tiger and Yakub

Memon, Dawood Ibrahim and other absconding accused were termed the 'archers', while the actual bomb planters were seen as mere tools in the hands of the real players. With this, the Supreme Court commuted the capital punishment for ten bomb planters to life imprisonment. Chaudhry was trying to use the same argument in court.

In another corner of the courtroom, a shy, unassuming sixty-four-year-old man was readying his arsenal. After all, Special Public Prosecutor Raja Thakare was too seasoned to be swayed by emotion. 'I am a practical man,' said an emphatic Thakare, straightening the *Criminal Manual* lying on the table—which he often referred to as a lawyer's bible. He dismissed Chaudhry's arguments as being good only in theory. To him, the convicts weren't 'delivery boys' or 'arrows'. They were 'merchants of death', and, hence, must be executed. He clarified quickly that he wasn't baying for anyone's blood, just that the planters and conspirators of these blasts deserved nothing but death.

Thakare was passionately arguing the point of view of over 100 policemen, all from the investigating agency formed to combat terror—the Anti-Terrorism Squad (ATS). These policemen had taken it upon themselves to bring the real perpetrators of the crime to book. Their investigation into the 7/11 blasts, and the court case that followed, had filled cupboard after cupboard in the court.

But the devil is always in the details. In the nine long years since the blasts, the investigations into the case have been repeatedly questioned. For one, the cops failed to clearly establish the role of the LeT or ISI in the blasts. Secondly, a home-grown terror outfit, the Indian Mujahideen (IM), has claimed responsibility for the blasts on several occasions since 2008. The trial has been peppered with allegations of torture by every single accused, something the police are already infamous for. But, above everything else, despite the investigation claiming to have busted the syndicate, no one knows who planted the bombs that went off in two locals, as only five planters were ever named or arrested.

Is this really an arrow that has hit the bullseye?

1

The Day Mumbai Derailed

At precisely 5.35 p.m., motorman Sachin Kumar Singh reported for duty at Churchgate railway station. Busy Tuesday, the ever-affable veteran of Mumbai's railways thought, casting a lazy glance around the station, the starting point of the Western Railway's suburban section. Located almost at the tip of south Mumbai, conveniently accessible from the region's commercial hub, Churchgate's evening rush was aggressive as always—commuters elbowing past others to grab a favourite window seat, rookies standing out in the crowd because of their inability to match that determined step into packed compartments, the regulars settling into animated chatter with their daily 'train groups', sharing snacks, others preparing to launch into bhajans or wearily discussing how the compartment only got more crowded every day.

Singh hung his satchel on a hook in his cabin. This was a Virar-bound fast train, scheduled to depart at 5.57 p.m. With thirty seconds to go, he buzzed the horn, a practice adopted by all railway motormen to warn people against boarding the train when it was about to leave. As the train picked up speed and the wind whistled in his ear, Singh focused on the grubby rail tracks ahead. Four stops later, as he slowed the train to a halt at Dadar station, it was 6.22 p.m. Well on time, Singh thought.

Two minutes later, as the train neared Matunga, Singh was nearly thrown off his feet by the loudest bang he had ever heard, a thundering boom that left his ears ringing. The impact was so visceral that it was a couple of moments before he could gather his bearings and pull the emergency brakes. The train hurtled forward for another 400 metres before it came to a grinding halt. By now, Singh was looking out into the back, eyes widening in disbelief and panic. A thick cloud of smoke hovered above one compartment, its walls torn, chunks of human flesh and mangled bodies lying on the tracks, as commuters from other compartments began jumping off the train, lurching, dazed, across the live railway tracks.

~

Nearly 70 lakh people hop on board a 'Mumbai local', as the suburban trains are referred to, every day. The network chiefly consists of a clutter of disorganized lines added to a showpiece of colonial mass transit planning. Sometimes decrepit, its tracks flooded annually during the monsoon, with its creaking infrastructure, the system somehow continues to function effectively enough for millions of Mumbaikars to call it the financial capital's lifeline.

In fact, the overcrowded trains actually trump the city's potholed roads and traffic snarls, and thousands of car owners occasionally leave their private vehicles at home to take a train and get to work on time. It's the busiest railway network in the world, the oldest in Asia. Whether it's a glitch in the overhead equipment or inundated tracks, when the Mumbai local is stalled, the megacity grinds to a halt.

Maybe that's why history shows us that the local trains have been an obvious terror target. Way back in 1998, a series of blasts at six locations in the central and western suburbs battered Mumbai's railway stations and trains, killing four people and injuring over thirty. The first wave of blasts was carried out over two consecutive days: in Kanjurmarg on 23 January, and Kandivali and Malad on 24 January. Three more blasts then occurred on 27 February near Virar, Santacruz and Kandivali railway stations.

The city hadn't yet forgotten the shock of the serial bomb blasts of 1993, in which 257 people died, so the 1998 train attacks seemed relatively insignificant.

In March 2003, terrorists struck the rail network again, this time blowing up a compartment of a Karjat-bound local train near the eastern suburb of Mulund, killing eleven and injuring seventy people. But again, despite the anger and outrage, railway commuters brushed aside their fear easily.

On 11 July 2006, that seemed impossible. The terrorists had come prepared to cause all the devastation they possibly could and the lifeline of the city was snuffed out, even if only for a few hours.

~

His ears still ringing, seized by a growing sense of dread, Singh jumped down from his cabin and raced towards the chaos. It was the general first-class compartment. The steel wall of the rake had been torn out. Mangled bodies lay in glistening pools of blood inside—shards of glass, parts of windows lay on the ground, seats and fans were crushed beyond recognition.

The stench of burning human flesh was unmistakable. As his hearing slowly returned, the first sounds he heard were of the survivors moaning.

Singh didn't know it then, but this was not the day's first bomb blast on the suburban railway network.

Just a minute earlier, at 6.23 p.m., another high-intensity explosion had taken place on the Borivali-bound fast train as it sped past Mahim railway station, just a few kilometres from Matunga. In fact, soon after the train left Dadar station, motorman Girishchandra Chaurasiya was informed that the train's motor-generator system had failed. Chaurasiya was still trying to understand what he had been told when the explosion took place. Coach no. 528A was destroyed by the explosion, its intensity so high that the roof of the platform was shattered, the wood on the iron benches outside was blown away.

Chaurasiya sent signals to the control room frantically, fearing that another speeding train would ram into them. This blast claimed forty-three lives and left ninety-six injured.

At the same time, another explosion was heard near Bandra station, also at 6.23 p.m.; once again, a first-class compartment had been targeted, this time on another Borivali-bound train.

Seconds later, one more explosion rocked the network, on a train between Bhayander and Mira Road stations, at 6.23 p.m., 42 kilometres from Churchgate, where the train had started. Station Superintendent Dinesh Chorge rushed out of his cabin on hearing the explosion. 'A cylinder blast, a stampede,' Chorge would later say, recalling his initial impressions. But, at the time, he could barely process his thoughts as he stood outside his office, unsure of what to do.

At 6.24 p.m., as Sachin Kumar Singh was trying to grapple with what had transpired on his train, a compartment exploded at Jogeshwari station. The train had just left the station, its last three bogies still near the platform when the bomb exploded.

At 6.25 p.m., a blast ripped apart another Borivali-bound train near the Khar subway. Senior Police Inspector Mohammad Salim Kadri, attached to the Government Railway Police (GRP), rushed to Khar after stopping at the blast site near Bandra. As he scrambled to help the victims, it was plainly obvious to Kadri that there was a pattern to the violence. Again, it was a first-class compartment, and again, the intensity of the explosion left no doubt that this was the work of professionals.

As locals joined Kadri in helping the injured, groups of volunteers carted victims across the tracks from where taxis, autorickshaws and private vehicles began taking them to Bhabha Hospital. The stationmaster, Nizamuddin, placed a call to the control room, voicing Kadri's thoughts. 'It is a terrorist attack.' When he hung up, he was taken aback by the urgency and panic in his own tone. In his twenty-one-year career, Nizamuddin had not seen anything like this.

The seventh and final bomb went off at 6.28 p.m. at Borivali railway station. Senior Inspector Satish Ahir would later recount seeing blood-soaked commuters lying on the ground. This bomb accounted for the maximum number of casualties among the seven explosions: 153 people were injured.

By the time policemen, initially confused by the multiple reports of a train explosion at different locations, reached the sites of devastation, commuters and slum dwellers living along the railway tracks had begun to ferry the dead and injured to hospitals. A disaster management plan existed on paper, but locals improvised in the absence of any clear directions. Posters were torn down to be used as makeshift stretchers, or as shrouds. Some slum dwellers dragged down the tarpaulin from their roofs to shield the dead lying in the darkness and rain.

Among the first journalists to reach Mahim railway station, Ritesh Uttamchandani, then a rookie photojournalist with the *Hindustan Times*, would later recollect the sense of disquiet hanging thick in the air, mingling with his own sense of unpreparedness on what he was witnessing. Having grown up in the quiet by-lanes of Mahim, visiting the station frequently with his father while on their way to the Gateway of India or to a garden in Charni Road, he had previously stood at the exact same spot dozens of times. But today, Mahim station was unrecognizable.

As he hurried in, he saw one body being carried out, then the second and then another. As he went deeper into the station, he saw part of the platform bathed in blood. Shaken, he began to shoot photos, alongside the other photojournalists who had arrived by then. An enraged mob charged at them, even assaulting a few men carrying camera lenses. The mood was darker than what Uttamchandani had expected. The journalists scattered and continued to gather data.

Elsewhere, in Khar and Santacruz too, the injured and the dead were being moved and the crowds at the blast sites were finally cleared. Each of the seven sites of the day's mayhem was cordoned off to make way for teams from the Forensic Science Laboratory, the Bomb Detection and Disposal Squad and the sniffer dog squad. Each team had to walk to the blast site—the railway services were snapped and millions of panicked commuters were on the roads, looking for a way to get home. The cell phone networks were jammed from the sudden pressure on them and the rumours floating around kept the city on edge.

By now, the rain was coming down in sheets. Water flowed into the affected compartments, taking with it crucial evidence on the nature of the explosion and the type of explosive used. The Forensic Science Laboratory teams worked at a feverish pace—collecting blood-soaked clothes, pieces of metal, soil, stones . . . Anything that could serve as evidence.

~

At the King Edward Memorial Hospital (KEM) in Parel, a neighbourhood formerly dotted with cotton mills that were now making way for swanky towers and office complexes, a group of medical interns was headed to the canteen for an evening snack when news of the explosions began to float in. The blasts had occurred long before Twitter and WhatsApp turned all news events into instant broadcasts; doctors in the midst of a busy evening dealing with monsoon-related ailments and other routine cases could not gauge the severity of the blasts when the first phone calls regarding an anticipated rush of victims came in.

But one look at the first victims being wheeled in and Dr Ravikant Singh, a twenty-five-year-old preparing for his post-graduation, knew immediately that this was going to be a dramatic evening, the most challenging one of his career perhaps.

Dr Singh was in the tiny 600 sq. ft casualty ward that was by now splattered with blood. At first, about a dozen victims were being treated, but within the next half hour, the casualty ward was flooded with patients. A small VIP suitcase in the casualty served as the 'disaster backup' for the municipality-run hospital's casualty ward, and within half an hour, the supply of syringes, gloves and atropine (a muscle relaxant) was all exhausted. Singh and the other interns were sent to sprint to every ward to collect the last available vial of atropine, critical to maintain the heart rate during surgery. They rummaged through the hospital storage units for essentials and rushed back with these to the casualty ward.

Meanwhile, patients continued to be wheeled in, bearing shrapnel injuries, some having lost too much blood, most unable to hear—all of them, without exception, in morbid fear, many still clutching cell phones trying to contact loved ones. As the evening wore on, another rush of visitors began, those looking for uncontactable family members. The crowds around hand-scrawled notices bearing the names of patients and the identified bodies grew restive.

A curious hitch arose amid the chaos: the doctors needed barbers urgently, to help shave areas on victims' bodies where surgical incisions had to be made, but there were only two present on duty. The number of doctors was insufficient too, given the hundreds of patients in the ward now. Two other doctors were called in for the emergency, and the resident doctors stepped up to the task. Then dean of the hospital, Dr Nilima Kshirsagar ordered gloves, syringes and other important medication to be purchased from private chemists outside the hospital. The chemists obliged too, arranging for supplies from elsewhere. In an hour, they made purchases worth Rs 2.5 lakh.

At Lokmanya Tilak Municipal General Hospital in Sion, nearly fifty bodies were brought in. Locally known as Sion Hospital, it was the only place with advanced medical facilities that was fairly close to the blast sites at Mahim and Bandra. Given its proximity to Dharavi, Asia's largest slum area, and the Eastern Express Highway, an important road connecting the south of the city to the eastern suburbs, the doctors were used to mass casualties. Cases of food poisoning, instances of scuffles breaking out between groups, and accidents were fairly common. The hospital boasted a disaster storeroom that housed emergency supplies for up to a hundred patients. As per protocol, a call from the casualty medical officer was all it took to mobilize all the resident doctors; this helped, as all of them were housed in a hostel inside the campus.

As in every disaster, victims with minor injuries were the first ones to crowd the hospitals. Sion Hospital dealt with a similar situation. The hospital, like many government-run facilities in Mumbai, lacked a good triage system to sort out patients according to the nature of their injuries.

By midnight, thankfully, the worst appeared to be over. Senior political leaders, including Prime Minister Manmohan Singh and Congress chief Sonia Gandhi, were announcing visits to the victims. Local Samaritans had pitched in with tea, biscuits and water for the doctors as well as for the crowds of relatives in the hospitals.

Outside, the train services had collapsed, their longest stoppage ever. Senior railway officials and police officers were in a huddle, keen to get the trains running to send out the message that Mumbai would not be cowed down. The roads were slow-moving streams of nervous and harried commuters hitching rides on buses, trucks and cars, as well as many simply resigned to walking all the way home. Local residents stepped out of their homes, with food and water, some offering shelter to the stranded.

The trauma phase was over, but these scars would not heal easily. Not for years.

2

The Aftermath

When Mumbai woke on 12 July 2006, the skies had cleared a little and the rains had eased. But neither was there respite for the city's crack terror investigators nor for the railway authorities who had just pulled an all-nighter, planning and executing the near-impossible task of clearing away the mangled reminders of the previous day's destruction. The trains, incredibly, had begun to run from the wee hours of the morning, but that Wednesday, the Western Railway line operated only 864 services, down from the daily 1039.

When, in 1993, the city's nerve centres, the commercial establishments, were targeted by terrorists through a set of well-positioned bombs in cars and scooters, the city bounced back quickly. This time, it appeared as if the attackers had hit dangerously close to home. The local trains, a part of the daily life of Mumbai's millions, seemingly symbolized the city's spirit—temporarily broken and struggling to get back on its feet.

The newspapers that morning reflected the city's despondence. 'Mumbai Attacked' cried the headline of *The*

Times of India. Popular tabloid *Mumbai Mirror* published a cover photograph of a severely injured victim, simply titled 'Stunned'. The newspapers and the strident television news coverage of the strikes deterred many from stepping out of home that day. The roads and railways were deserted that morning.

Those who stepped out were suspicious and jumpy, calling police controls to report every unclaimed object in a train—from forgotten lunch boxes to discarded plastic bags. Schools and colleges, sensing the anxiety among students and parents, stayed shut for the day. The municipality headquarters near the iconic Chhatrapati Shivaji Terminus (CST) railway station saw only 60 per cent of its staff in attendance. Mantralaya, the administrative headquarters of the state government of Maharashtra, witnessed a turnout of 50 per cent. Dog squads were kept busy all day at all major railway stations, while the railways made announcements urging commuters to stay alert and report any suspicious objects or movements.

When the 5.57 p.m. Virar fast left that evening from Churchgate station, there was a deathly hush.

Meanwhile, frantic calls were exchanged as rumours circulated about supposed blasts elsewhere. In a bus in the eastern suburb of Ghatkopar, another one in the western suburb of Borivali, one in Kharghar in the satellite township of Navi Mumbai—they were all hoaxes. Television news channels began to chase police authorities and intelligence agencies, hoping to coax out some information regarding the motive and the perpetrators.

The first morsel of news was suitably alarming. Four members of the Students Islamic Movement of India (SIMI), an extremist organization banned in 2001, had gone missing from Solapur. Suspicious investigators formed a team and an alert was sent out to track the four.

Other police teams began to record statements, several hundreds of them. Victims in hospitals, witnesses at railway stations, anyone in a position to speak about the previous evening's insanity was welcome, but barring a few odd theories and suspicions, investigators had no specific leads to work with on the morning after. It seemed as though the attackers who walked into the crowded railway station and boarded packed trains had simply vanished into thin air.

The probe was transferred to the Anti-Terrorism Squad (ATS). Seven teams were formed, each consisting of six policemen. By late evening, relying solely on a network of informers, the investigators had one lead—fourteen men had executed the blasts. But they could not trace a link between what happened on 11 July 2006 to any of the recent blasts. The 1993 blasts were the handiwork of the Mumbai underworld; a SIMI faction executed the Ghatkopar, Vile Parle, Mulund and Mumbai Central explosions of 2002–03; the Gujarat Muslim Revenge Force was responsible for the Gateway of India and Zaveri Bazaar blasts during the same time. Who were these fourteen men? Whom did they owe their allegiance to? Who funded this mindless violence targeted at innocents? The ATS was left grappling with these questions in the dark.

One thought nudged ATS chief K.P. Raghuvanshi forward. He recalled arresting thirty-seven-year-old Mushiruddin Siddiqui and twenty-eight-year-old Manzoor Ansari on 30 January that year. They'd arrived from Nepal and were nabbed at the Kurla terminus. The duo was carrying 950 grams of a powder explosive, along with maps of Mumbai and Maharashtra. In fact, on the basis of the information provided by Siddiqui, two huge consignments of weapons and explosives had been seized in the past few months. This time, however, Siddiqui did not have the answers.

~

The King Edward Memorial Hospital, Sion, Bhabha and Bhagwati hospitals remained a hub of activity through the day; families milled around the morgues, wards and ICUs, hoping to find a loved one who had gone missing after the blasts. At Sion Hospital, doctors decided to take photographs of all the dead so that relatives could be shown these pictures on a computer screen instead of the stomach-churning reality of the morgue. Each body was cleaned, then photographed. Dr Meena Kumar who was responsible then for managing the trauma care facility would remember later how this little procedure saved families from having to search among rows of mutilated bodies for a familiar face.

Amidst the thousands of such distraught visitors was the family of Sub-inspector Suresh Pawar. Posted at the passport office in Worli, Pawar had resumed work only a week ago, having taken time off to mourn his mother's death.

On 11 July, Pawar was travelling with a friend who alighted at Dadar station, having been summoned back to work. Pawar had continued his journey on one of the ill-fated trains. His family searched at three hospitals, before finally finding his body at Bhabha Hospital in Bandra. It was Pawar's twenty-one-year-old son who recognized his father's corpse—he was still wearing his police-issued khaki socks and belt. While Pawar's body was identified without much difficulty, many others awaited the results of DNA tests, for there were several bodies mutilated beyond recognition.

At the sites of the carnage, railway employees continued the mammoth task of clearing the remains of the trains. At midday in Khar, forty workers were removing pieces of metal lodged in the tracks, repeating the laborious task they'd completed at the other sites. Supervisors pushed them to work longer, harder, faster. Everybody agreed by then that if Mumbai had to return to normalcy, the train services had to be fully restored.

~

Wednesday also saw Advocate Jamshed Mistry, the counsel for Dr Sarosh Mehta, moving the Bombay High Court for a hearing on the safety lapses and the gaps in tackling the emergency situation at the railway stations. Dr Mehta, an orthopaedist, had taken up the cause of government accountability in providing immediate medical attention on the railways after he witnessed a brutal railway accident in 2001. The 7/11 explosions had shone the spotlight on these lacunae.

Minutes after the blasts, confusion had reigned at the railway stations. The helpline numbers failed to provide any useful information to frantic callers. Not only were citizens frustrated, but several injured also had to suffer delays in availing treatment, owing to the lack of professional expertise and organized, systemic support. The court had earlier instructed the railways to arrange for the victims' travel and hospitalization in the event of such a crisis, but on 7/11 it was again the bystanders and Good Samaritans who stepped up to this task.

Meanwhile, as the day ended, the investigating agencies named the first suspect organization: the Lashkar-e-Taiba (LeT). Some intelligence officers also believed that Pakistani actors may have plotted the carnage in retaliation to the troubles in the Pakistani province of Balochistan. Pakistan had been accusing the premier Indian intelligence agency, the Research and Analysis Wing (RAW), of stoking the fires in the region. If Pakistan wanted to teach India a lesson, the attacks on the Mumbai trains seemed like the perfect method. But without specific leads, these were just theories.

Then, late that night, there was a significant breakthrough in New Delhi. Aijaz Hussain, arrested from the Jangpura locality earlier that year, informed the Delhi Police that an LeT operative who had been working in Mumbai for the past few months was responsible for the blasts. Originally from Kashmir, the operative had used several aliases during the course of his stay in the city, one of which was Mohammed.

Hussain said he did not know the operative's real name, but he had a phone number that was allegedly his. He claimed to have acted only as a link between the undercover operative and his senior in the LeT in Pakistan, Mukhtar Ahmed. He also confessed to supplying explosives and money to various LeT operatives in the Valley on several occasions, on Ahmed's instructions.

Despite these admissions, Hussain denied having played a role in the Mumbai blasts. Instead, he blamed the missing Kashmiri for the diabolical plot hatched ostensibly over the several months that he'd been living in Mumbai. Over the last four months, Hussain had passed on over Rs 3 crore to the operative, the money sent from Ahmed in Pakistan.

Those in the ATS privy to this valuable piece of information could hardly sleep that night. Their target had just been set: they had to find the missing Kashmiri. The route to finding him was complicated; Hussain had led them into a tangled web to help track the operative, and they could well spend months unravelling the threads before they could locate their man.

3

The Good Life

Rewind
March 2001

Scores of Muslims across the country read with rapt attention as newspapers splashed images of a Quran burning in Delhi. A few from the right wing animatedly cheered and shouted slogans around the fire as they protested against the Taliban destroying the iconic Bamiyan Buddha statues, which were built in 507 CE, in Afghanistan.

SIMI, an Islamic youth organization, gained prominence during this time. After the Quran-burning incident, SIMI volunteers were accused of inciting riots in several parts of the country. Fourteen people died and twenty-four were injured in Kanpur, an industrial town in northern India and home to a large population of Muslims. The police arrested as many as 286 people and recovered 112 weapons, including country-made pistols, bombs, cartridges and knives. In western India, a mob of 150 young men went on a rampage in Pune's Ganj Peth area, burning vehicles, forcibly shutting down shops and attacking those people who had stepped out of their homes. The police detained fifty men and eventually arrested twenty-two.

Four months later, on 30 July 2001, four men—two each from the SIMI and the Hizb-ul-Mujahideen, a terrorist organization from Jammu and Kashmir—were arrested by the Special Cell of the Delhi Police. The police recovered 2 kilograms of RDX, 6 kilograms of other explosives, 2.5 litres of nitrobenzene oil, a grenade launcher, grenade shells, electronic detonators, remote-controlled devices and a wireless set, among other things that could be used to make bombs. It was a year of unrest in India.

SIMI, the group that had been implicated in the year-long violence, had come into existence on 25 April 1977 in Aligarh Muslim University. It was the youth wing of the pre-Independence Jamaat-e-Islami Hind (JIH), an Islamic organization. In 1993, SIMI broke away from the JIH, after the organization went from rooting for a state based on the sharia, the Islamic law, to fighting for the rights of Muslims as a minority in a secular country. SIMI's objectives were clear: they believed in governing human life on the basis of the Quran, the propagation of Islam, jihad (religious war) for the cause of Islam and, most importantly, the 'destruction of nationalism and the establishment of an Islamic Caliphate in India'. Its strategy included inducting students in the organization and using them to propagate of Islam and to mobilize support for jihad.

The same year, the terror attack on the World Trade Center in the United States renewed focus on Islamic extremism—not only in the US, but around the world. In India too, the police cracked down on unlawful activities, detaining many Muslims across the country. SIMI was already a troublemaker for the BJP-led Indian government. So when SIMI leaders adopted a pro-Taliban stand during public discourses, they were swiftly banned by the government.

~

On 27 September 2001, around 7 p.m., the phone rang at the local SIMI office in Kurla, a predominantly Muslim area in Mumbai. 'SIMI *ko ban kar diya hai*. Office *bandh karo aur niklo* (SIMI has been banned. Shut the office and leave),' said a voice on the phone, curtly. Civil engineer and SIMI president Irshad Khan banged the receiver down and looked around anxiously. Volunteers and local youngsters who came to the SIMI library every day crowded the office. Khan decided not to heed the urgent phone call and refused to announce to the packed office that the government had banned SIMI only three hours ago.

Within an hour, the Kurla police barged into the office and arrested nine people, including SIMI volunteers Ehtesham Siddiqui and Tanveer Ansari. Ehtesham was studying chemical engineering at Narayan Nagu Patil Engineering College in Raigad at the time, while Tanveer was a certified Unani doctor working with the Muslim Ambulance Society Maternity and Nursing Home. The police seized books on Islam, and later used that as evidence of SIMI's 'anti-national' and unlawful activities. The following day, a magistrate granted bail to all nine, including Ehtesham and Tanveer, as the correct procedure was not followed by the police.

Once an organization is banned, the local police put up a notification outside its premises. But in this case, the arrests were made before a notification could be put up. Locals from the area gathered in court to protest against the 'illegal arrests.'

As the nine accused walked out, the sloganeering became even more intense and the police made more arrests. They took a taxi driver, a banana vendor and Irshad Khan into custody again. The courts took a month to grant bail to Irshad this time and another fourteen years to acquit him of all the charges.

To spread word of the ban and dissuade people from joining the organization, the police finally put up copies of the ban notification at places of congregation, like madrasas, the local mosques and at police chowkis. Assistant Sub-inspector Vijay Mandlik, from the Kurla police station, accompanied by other police officers, also announced the ban on the streets, using a megaphone. He was met with intense stares in Kurla, which was a hotbed of crime. He finally visited the SIMI office and sealed it shut.

By 2008, SIMI had been branded a terror outfit, with more than ninety-one cases against its volunteers and arrests of 351 of its members in the state of Maharashtra.

~

All this while, in Pune's Mominpura area, twenty-four-year-old Faisal Atta-ur Rahman Shaikh could not stop picturing the holy Quran going up in flames. SIMI's teachings echoed in his mind: jihad is the only way to counter the atrocities against Muslims and establish the supremacy of Islam.

It had taken Faisal several years to reach this point. Dusky and sturdily built, he was born to a middle-class family in Mumbai. His father worked in Saudi Arabia as the head of a petrol pump's maintenance department. As a child, Faisal moved between Mumbai, Malegaon and Pune. The years he spent in the madrasa till he reached class ten had a huge impact on him. His father insisted that his children not only do well academically, but also be grounded in religious tenets. Everyone noticed the change in Faisal, a quiet youngster, over time. From his immediate family to his relatives, he would compel everyone to immerse themselves in prayer. His cousins would quickly pull down their veils when he walked into the room.

After Faisal took his class eleven exams, his father sent him to Pune to live with an uncle, and study for a diploma in electronics. Faisal resisted—he was keen on starting a business of his own, but his father insisted he do a course in engineering. With absolutely no inclination to study further, Faisal failed the first year of the course. He started doing odd jobs to sustain himself. The frustration to prove himself only grew with time.

For a short while, he worked at Cheema Transport Company in Pune's Kondhwa area. Then he started a garment business, buying clothes from Mumbai and selling them in Pune. After his father moved back from Saudi Arabia, his entire family, including his two younger brothers, Rahil and Muzzammil Atta-ur Rahman Shaikh, shifted to Pune from Mumbai's Mira Road. His youngest brother, Muzzammil, was still in school, while Rahil, a computer hardware engineer, had a steady job. In Pune, Faisal strove to find a steady income but failed. Faisal also refused to marry; he wanted to prove himself before he got to that stage.

In the year 2000, the family moved to a bigger house in Mominpura, a congested Muslim area in Pune, known for its scrumptious food during Ramadan. And it was at Mecca Mosque in Mominpura that Faisal found his inspiration. The pastel-green-and-white-coloured three-storey facade had a striking portico with a public announcement system attached to the first floor that wouldn't allow anyone living in the vicinity to miss their prayers. During his visits to the mosque, Faisal would sit for the biweekly programmes organized by

SIMI members. He would listen to older members guide the young Muslims who came to the mosque. As the sun set, and the lilting sound of the azan rang from the megaphone at the entrance of the mosque, they would tell young minds about the atrocities committed against Muslims in India and the world. They would tell gruesome stories of the destruction of the Babri Masjid and the riots in Mumbai. Faisal became concerned about the plight of his Muslim brothers; he now wanted revenge for what had happened in the past.

Faisal immersed himself in religious literature, and made religion a tool to overcome his insignificant past. His knowledge of the Hadiths (sayings and traditions of the Holy Prophet) baffled his social circle. The twenty-six-year-old took pride in hanging out at the 400 sq. ft SIMI office in Pune, the cultural capital of Maharashtra, before and after the official ban on the organization. Faisal had the gait of a prominent SIMI member even though he wasn't an office bearer or a SIMI volunteer yet. Outside the mosque, Faisal would spearhead discussions on Islam, and take centre stage in telling local boys about atrocities against Muslims.

But Faisal was himself still a young man. He still frequented bars and clubs, looking for the company of women. Despite being a chain-smoker, he was a teetotaller. He was so paranoid about being tricked into having liquor that he carried a packed bottle of water every time he went to a club. Faisal would sport a colourful baseball cap when he wasn't wearing his skullcap. He liked dressing stylishly and his youthful looks hid the budding religious fanatic within. He was the perfect target for a terror outfit—fearless and pessimistic, with an inclination for following instructions blindly.

One evening in October, Faisal talked of revenge. His voice echoed in the ears of the people in his group, including other SIMI regulars, like thirty-five-year-old Suhail Mehmood Shaikh and twenty-two-year-old Rizwan Dawrey, Faisal's closest friend in Pune. The thin and frail-looking Suhail was the oldest SIMI activist in the mosque. Both Suhail and Dawrey agreed with Faisal. Revenge, they believed, was the only way to fight the holy war for the cause of Islam. But for revenge, Faisal knew he needed training. And he knew where to get that training: Pakistan. He was, after all, going to live 'the good life'.

Through his SIMI contacts, Faisal approached Abdul Kumbhar, who travelled often to Pakistan to meet his sister, Sharifa. Faisal convinced Kumbhar to take him along on his next visit. On 23 June 2001, Faisal and Kumbhar reached Delhi to apply for a visa at the Pakistani consulate. Kumbhar, who had travelled to Pakistan earlier, got his visa, but the consulate rejected Faisal's application. Disappointed, he returned to Pune, but decided to reapply for the visa. Three months later, Faisal was on a flight to Pakistan.

~

As soon as Faisal landed in Pakistan, he called up Abu Harkat of the Markaz-ud-Dawa-wal-Irshad, a terrorist organization later renamed Jama'at-ud-Da'wah (JuD). Its armed wing was called Lashkar-e-Taiba, literally 'army of the pure'. Abu Harkat agreed to meet Faisal at his office in Lahore. But Faisal's determination seemed to falter.

I am not alone in this; it's the path of Allah, Faisal reminded himself as he faced the single-storey bungalow with a courtyard, where he was scheduled to meet Abu Harkat. Faisal introduced himself to the security guard manning the front door and was let in. 'You've come to the right place,' Abu Harkat said, welcoming him. After a brief chat Abdul Razzak, another recruit from Hyderabad, a southern Indian town, led him to a dormitory.

Razzak, a recruit from the late 1990s, sensed Faisal's apprehension. Speaking in a mix of Hindi and Urdu, he said, 'You are of no good use if you are untrained. Training is a must.' Hearing Razzak's familiar language, Faisal was reassured. Jihad was his only chance of doing something worthwhile in his life, he thought.

The 'haven' Faisal had reached was built by Hafeez Saeed. Saeed was the amir (spiritual leader) of JuD. He was born in Punjab, in Pakistan, and was a lecturer at a university in Lahore until the 1980s, when he left for Saudi Arabia to support terrorists fighting the Soviet Union in Afghanistan. He returned to Pakistan and formed an Islamic movement, with followers of the Ahl-e-Hadith sect of Islam. This movement later led to the formation of the LeT, with Zaki-ur-Rehman Lakhvi as its co-founder and chief military commander. One of the second-rung commanders of this very organization would play a pivotal role in Faisal's life.

~

The following day, Faisal left for Karachi with Razzak. A man in his sixties, with a long white beard, received them in Karachi and took Faisal to a bungalow on Tipu Sultan Road. The bungalow's owner, Arif Qasmani, a millionaire businessman and commander with the LeT, met Faisal and asked him to stay the night, sharing a room with some other Pakistanis. The next day, Razzak spoke to Qasmani on Faisal's behalf. When Razzak explained that Faisal wanted to train and fight in India, Qasmani was prompt to ask, 'You know the training is tough. Are you ready for the drill?'

Eight days later, Faisal reached the Al-Aqsa training camp, in the hilly terrain of Muzaffarabad, the capital of Pakistan-occupied Kashmir (PoK). The camp had a huge training ground in the centre, surrounded by trees. There was a mosque with tents erected on the periphery for the recruits. Faisal followed the fixed schedule of the two-day camp: Fajr namaz (morning prayers) at 5 a.m., Quran khani (recitation) at 6 a.m., breakfast at 8 a.m., followed by the Zuhr (morning) and Asr (afternoon) namaz at 1 p.m. Then firing practice, followed by Maghrib (evening) namaz. The day ended with lectures goading and cajoling the new recruits to become fidayeen (an extremist ready to sacrifice himself) and achieve martyrdom. In a few days, Faisal was introduced to the handling of TT revolvers, AK-47s and pistols. He also learnt the basics of assembling bombs that could kill hundreds at a time.

Soon after the training, Faisal and Razzak headed to Lahore for an LeT event, attended by the who's who of the LeT machinery. Faisal could only identify Qasmani, but noticed that the man next to Qasmani looked important and commanded the same authority as Qasmani. He wondered who the man was.

The next day Faisal met Azam Cheema, the important-looking person from the LeT event. Faisal instantly liked the 6.5-foot-tall Cheema, who patted Faisal's back with appreciation. He makes you feel like his own, Faisal thought. He smiled as he recalled working for Cheema Transport Company back home in Pune. What a coincidence, he thought. In the days to come, Cheema was going to be Faisal's mentor.

Cheema handed a bundle of notes to Faisal. 'Send more people like you to Pakistan for training,' he was told. As he prepared for his journey back home, Qasmani handed over some utensils, clothes and the visiting card of a shop in Delhi.

'With this luggage and money, no one will question you at the border. Reach Delhi and hand over the visiting card to its owner. He will give you Rs 20,000.'

Two days later, Faisal entered India through the Wagah border and headed to the shop in Delhi to collect his money. As promised, no questions were asked.

On coming back home, Faisal animatedly described his trip to his younger brothers, who seemed equally excited by his experience. The first instalment of money through hawala had flowed in just four months after Faisal had returned. Rahil and Faisal had come to Mumbai from Pune to collect Rs 1,80,000 from one of Cheema's men. Finally, he thought, he would have the life he had always imagined for himself. He was no longer a failure. He felt strong and powerful. He was a Lashkar-e-Taiba recruit, a man who was going to command a major offensive against India.

4

Maximum Damage

February 2006

From the dingy room in Pune's Mominpura, Faisal had certainly moved up in life. He now lived in one of Mumbai's fanciest suburbs: Bandra. Even non-locals recognize this locality, for it houses Bollywood's favourite Khans. And it also has the beautiful Carter Road promenade that sees Bandra's elite come out every morning in branded sportswear for a jog, running past young lovers canoodling in their own little corners, gazing at the waves against the rising sun.

For a man in search of both anonymity and solace just before his biggest mission, this setting was perfect. Faisal rented out a compact, but pretty, terrace apartment on Perry Cross Road's Lucky Villa, only a couple of hundred metres away from Carter Road. He assumed a different identity—he called himself Sameer now, and his neighbours never saw too much of him. The only ones who did see him occasionally were a bunch of young boys playing football in a ground nearby. Faisal was often spotted staring at them from his little window.

Was he taken with their spirit? Or was he looking at them through the lens of a 'talent-hunter'? After all, Cheema's cold voice berating him for not sending enough men to Pakistan for training still rang in his ears.

But this incident was in 2004. A lot had changed in the last two years. The first time he had visited Pakistan was five years ago. And even though Cheema had supposedly seen a certain spark in the young Faisal, the going was anything but easy for him.

In fact, during one of his visits to Pakistan in 2004, he had almost given up on the idea of returning to India. He wanted to settle down in the neighbouring country. But Cheema wouldn't have any of it. 'Something big is being planned for Mumbai. And you are my man to make it happen,' Cheema had said.

Whatever it was in Cheema's tone, whether it was encouragement, a threat or a warning, it pushed Faisal to fly back to India to carry out the 'big plan'. But it was jinxed from the very beginning. He ended up leaving his passport at a check post while entering Pakistan from the Iran–Pakistan border. But Cheema promptly arranged for a new passport to be delivered to him—a Pakistani one where he was identified as Mohammad Akram. Along with it a visa for Saudi Arabia for performing Umrah, a holy pilgrimage for Muslims, was also delivered. Since Faisal's brother Rahil and his friend Rizwan Dawrey lived in Saudi Arabia, it seemed like it would all work out.

But there was another stroke of bad luck on his way back from Mecca. Faisal was frisked at a checkpoint. While he claimed to be a Pakistani citizen, the officers found an Indian driver's licence on him. He was jailed for three days and deported back to India on an emergency visa.

Even though Faisal managed to wriggle out of these sticky situations, he had learnt from his mistakes. He knew this time there was no room for carelessness. After all, this is what Cheema had been preparing him for all these years. And now the orders had come.

'Get to work. Select targets that will lead to maximum damage. Mumbai *mein badi vardat karni hai* (We have to do something big in Mumbai).' It was time for Faisal to prove his worth.

The orders were not Cheema's alone. He was the architect of the plan in India but no operation in the LeT is executed without the will of its founders and commanders, Hafeez Saeed and Zaki-ur-Rehman Lakhvi, who are hand in glove with India's biggest foreign enemy: the Inter-Services Intelligence (ISI).

~

Days later, six SIMI men sat in a circle with Faisal in his living room. At the centre, a copy of the holy Quran was placed. One of the men in the room, Asif Bashir Khan, known more commonly by his alias, Junaid, was the ex-president of SIMI's Jalgaon branch. A civil engineer by profession, Asif was battling several criminal charges, including that of sending two young men to Kashmir. He was the sharpest of them all.

Then there was Ehtesham Siddiqui, once charged for being the man behind SIMI's inciting literature. Hailing from Azamgarh, the publisher would later be known as the 'RTI [Right to Information] man', who used replies from RTI applications to prepare his defence in court. Ehtesham had never visited Pakistan for training and wanted to strengthen SIMI activities through training within India. He even visited plots near Nepal to see if they could be converted into training camps, but he had dropped the idea temporarily. Asif, Ehtesham and Faisal knew each other through SIMI gatherings.

Tanveer Ansari, the Unani doctor arrested along with Ehtesham from the SIMI Kurla office, now worked at the M.H. Saboo Siddique Maternity and General Hospital. Tanveer had worked at Prince Aly Khan Hospital in the past. He had also headed SIMI's Mira Road office and attended a training camp in Pakistan after Ehtesham convinced him in 2004.

The fourth man was Suhail Mehmood Shaikh from Pune, who had dabbled in SIMI activities in the past and knew Asif. The fifth was Zameer Latifur Rehman Shaikh, a thirty-year-old taxi driver, who had met Tanveer in Kurla and had consulted him during his wife's pregnancy. The sixth person was Faisal's youngest brother, Muzzammil.

Except Asif and Faisal, no one knew the reason for the meeting. Speaking from the circle, Asif said, looking deep into each person's eyes, 'Faisal has received the message. It's time. It's time to seek justice for our brothers.' Faisal nodded in agreement. Though he had an advantage over the rest because of his connection to Cheema, he relied on Asif to get things going. Asif was a powerful orator and people obeyed his commands. 'Start looking for targets. Targets that will cause maximum damage,' Asif ordered. No one dared to ask any questions.

The brainstorming session began. Each of them began thinking out loud, naming places they thought would be perfect to attack. Cinema halls, shopping arcades, government offices—they named all the places where large crowds were bound to gather. In an hour, they had already shortlisted potential targets. The list included the Bombay Stock Exchange (BSE) on Dalal Street, World Trade Centre (WTC) in Cuffe

Parade, Siddhivinayak temple in Prabhadevi, Mahalaxmi temple near Haji Ali, along with two of the biggest and busiest shopping malls in the city: High Street Phoenix in Lower Parel and Inorbit Mall in Goregaon. Asif picked Faisal, Suhail and Zameer to carry out a detailed assessment of these shortlisted locations. He felt that Zameer, who drove a taxi for a living, would be an asset in the process given his knowledge of the city's roads.

But before a plan could be signed and sealed, the discussion was interrupted by a knock on the door. 'Who the hell is it?' a displeased Asif thundered. Faisal, who had just opened the door, introduced the man as Mohammad Alam Qureshi, his best friend. A cloth retailer from Mira Road, Qureshi often hung out with Faisal at local dance bars—Chembur's Discovery Dance Bar was their favourite.

'We don't have to worry about him,' insisted Faisal, escorting him inside. After all, Faisal had told Qureshi everything—his visits to Pakistan, his training in the LeT camps and the financial support he had received from Cheema.

Before Asif could make up his mind about how much he could trust this uninvited visitor, it was time for namaz. The men, including Qureshi, cleansed themselves, prayed and formed a circle once again. It was time to take the oath. Asif asked everyone to place their hands on the Quran and made a call for jihad. He asked everyone to promise on the holy book that the discussion would be kept a secret. But Qureshi refused to take the oath. He knew little about their discussions and what had taken place in the room, he argued.

Later, Qureshi turned out to be the only key witness to the conspiracy meetings.

~

The next morning, the group began their reconnaissance. The idea was to blend in with the crowds, without raising the needle of suspicion. The first spot they surveyed was the BSE, Asia's oldest securities market. The brokers here deal in hundreds of crores in a single day, trading shares of more than 5000 companies.

Earlier, before this giant building was built in 1975, brokers used to gather under banyan trees in the area to conduct their business. That year, the BSE was established as the Native Share & Stock Brokers' Association. But Faisal and Co. seemed to have forgotten the darkest moment in the BSE's otherwise glorious timeline—12 March 1993. That day a powerful car bomb had exploded in the basement of the BSE, severely damaging the twenty-eight-storey building and killing more than fifty people.

Thirteen years after the blasts, the BSE continues to be guarded like a fortress. A simple survey of the tight security at the entry points to the building alone told them that attacking the BSE was out of question.

The trio surveyed the WTC next. Built by the wealthy Parsi real-estate scion Shapoorji Pallonji, the WTC was the tallest building in Mumbai at one point in time. However, the building had lost its charm over the years and now it attracted crowds only during the few exhibitions that were held over there. Yet, it boasted of a good security set-up and had to be dropped from the list of targets.

Next on the terror list was the Siddhivinayak temple. Unlike most temples, where people move around freely and security is limited, Siddhivinayak is heavily protected. Until the 1980s, only a few people frequented the temple for darshan. But things changed when Bollywood superstar Amitabh Bachchan met with a near-fatal accident on the sets of *Coolie* in 1983. His wife, who was also an actress, Jaya Bachchan, reportedly began visiting the temple to pray for her husband's recovery. When he was finally discharged, he offered a gold crown to the Ganesha idol in the temple. As the years went by, visiting the temple before any big event became an unwritten norm for a huge section of the rich and famous in town. By 2006, the trust that owns and runs the temple had already spent Rs 5 crore on CCTV cameras, metal detectors and baggage scanners. Work on a blast-proof security wall was under way. Another terror target had to be taken off the list.

The other temple on their list, the Mahalaxmi temple, didn't boast of crowds large enough, despite its popularity, for the damage Cheema had in mind. If this temple was going to be the target, it would have to be bombed during Navaratri, a nine-day Hindu festival celebrated in October. The two shopping malls were taken off the list too as they had tight security. The month-long exercise had not borne any fruit— not one chosen target fit the bill.

The group then decided to scan for other possible targets. They travelled across the city, including its suburbs, in the local trains, in the hope of finding a spot that was crowded, but not heavily guarded. They started early in the morning. Each of them travelled multiple times on the Central, Western and Harbour railway routes that divide Mumbai's rail network. And then realization struck them—there was no security at the railway stations or in the trains; no scanners, no metal detectors, nothing at all.

That night, the trio assembled at Bandra railway station. Faisal looked at the sea of people entering and exiting the busy station. *Maximum damage*—he rolled the words over in his mind. He now knew his target. It would only be a matter of hours before he communicated his target to his handlers back in Pakistan.

5

The Terror Trail

'*Mubaraka* (congratulations),' an excited caller exclaimed on the phone. The call was received in Dhaka, Bangladesh, and was made from Karachi, in Pakistan. This call, just a day after the deadly attacks, was one among the thousands of calls intercepted by the Indian Intelligence Bureau (IB). The mission had been accomplished and a congratulatory message was in order. Another call traced by the central agencies directed the police to a public call office (PCO) in Juhu, Mumbai's posh waterfront suburb. This was not a work call; it seemed to be a personal one as the voices were filled with emotion. The police recorded the call, which was a hurried conversation between a mother and a son. It seemed like an anxious mother in Karachi was relieved to hear that her son was doing fine in Mumbai.

These calls raised the police's suspicions that foreign organizations were involved in the mayhem that had ensued in Mumbai. Soon, a PCO owner approached the Mumbai Police with more information. Three calls were made from his telephone booth to Karachi, Dubai and Aurangabad. Investigators continued to track more such suspicious calls from the western suburbs of Borivali and Malad to Afghanistan and Pakistan; some of these calls were made minutes before the first bomb went off. Most of the tapped calls recorded conversations about an accomplished mission. Another eerie thought struck the investigators when they analysed the locations of the target: had the bomb planters watched the aftermath of the attacks from a safe distance? To make it harder to track the callers, several telephone booths in different locations had been used to throw the investigators off-track. The handlers, who the police now believed sat across the border, used satellite phones, and most calls were routed through a third country. The only way to get a lead was by tracing all suspicious phone calls until at least thirty days before the incident.

Three months before the train blasts, several hoax calls were received on the Western and Central railway lines, as the planners prepared their final assault. The ATS found out later that the terrorists were carrying out mock drills to confuse the investigators.

During any police investigation, there are hits and misses. Every government agency tried adding new information. Aijaz Hussain, who was arrested by the Delhi Police, was one such 'miss'. Initially the revelations he had made seemed vital, but the ATS soon reached a dead end following his lead. Also, by the third day there was so much irrelevant information and so many different theories floating around that it seemed as though most of them were a hoax.

Unlike in the past, Lady Luck was not being kind to the investigating agency this time. In March 1993, the police had managed to crack the serial-blasts case within twenty-four hours because of an explosive-laden Maruti found at Worli and an RDX-laden scooter at Dadar that had led the police to the kingpin of the attacks, Tiger Memon. This time there were no easy clues available.

The ATS geared up for the probe and allotted two senior officers to supervise field investigations. ATS chief K.P. Raghuvanshi's instructions to his officers were clear—food, family and fun had to take a back seat. 'Locals are involved in the blasts. Track them,' Raghuvanshi told his men. Besides the ATS, the case was also being investigated by the Crime Branch, a unit of the Mumbai Police believed to have a better network of informers; the Special Branch, another unit of the Mumbai Police; the GRP; and intelligence agencies. By now eighteen teams, of fifty officers each, were trying to hunt down the local bomb planters, many of whom the investigators believed were members of the banned SIMI. The police began combing operations in Muslim-dominated areas like Malwani, Mumbra, Shivaji Nagar and Mira Road. The operations were intense, with the police picking up 200 men for questioning from Malwani alone. While thirteen people were asked to stay back, the rest were allowed to go home with bruised bodies. Facing harrowing questions from the media and their own bosses, investigators even considered the possibility of India's most wanted criminal, Dawood Ibrahim, playing a role in the blasts. But that turned out to be another dead end.

In car sheds along the tracks, mangled remains of the train coaches continued to tell the ghastly story of the terror strike. The team of forensic experts studying the evidence suggested that RDX was used in the bombs with pencil or electrical timers. When clubbed with nitro chloride, RDX is capable of destroying heavy metal. The police also believed that all the timers were set for 6.30 p.m., but a slight error in judgement eventually led to the bombs going off one after another.

RDX had been used twice in the past: once in the 1993 serial blasts and then in the 2003 twin blasts at the Gateway of India and Zaveri Bazaar in Mumbai. RDX was commonly routed through Nepal and Bangladesh, and concealed in boxes of computer hardware, fruits and vegetables. This RDX found its way to the Marathwada region of Maharashtra, whose districts, including Aurangabad and Jalna, were slowly becoming a hotbed of suspicious activities. The police believed that SIMI members had made Marathwada their home after being driven away from other parts of the state following the ban in 2001. They believed that sleeper cells were active in the region too.

In May 2006, two months before the blasts, the ATS had discovered a large quantity of RDX in Aurangabad and Malegaon. The police seized 43 kilograms of RDX, sixteen AK-47 rifles, 3200 live cartridges and sixteen magazines of AK-47 rifles, and 50 hand grenades but state intelligence officers suspected that at least 1000 kilograms of RDX had been smuggled into India and stored in the Marathwada belt. A large part of this could have been used in the terror strike on 7/11.

At the time of the arms haul, the meaning of what had seemed like a senseless communication, via email, was now suddenly clear. *'Bachey ki delivery ho gayi hai. Maa khairiyat se hai.* (The baby has been delivered and the mother is fine.)' *'Shaadi ki tarikh tay ho gayi thi, magar use postpone karna pada.* (The wedding date had been finalized, but it had to be postponed.)'

The investigators realized that these emails referred to the delivery of the explosives that had landed in Aurangabad. These exchanges were between Sayyed Akif, an LeT operative, and Zabiuddin Ansari. Ansari, who hailed from Marathwada, had been on the run since May 2006. Years later, he would be accused of giving instructions to the assailants, along with three others from LeT's control room in Karachi, during the

26/11 Mumbai attacks in 2008, under the alias of Abu Jundal. The emails contained coded information about a possible attack on an Indian city. The messages, decoded by the ATS, also suggested that the date for the operation was fixed, but had to be postponed for a variety of reasons. But this was all the ATS could find against Ansari in connection with the train blasts and he was later dropped as a suspect.

The ATS teams in Mumbai had now reached Kalyan, Thane and Navi Mumbai to question dealers of gelatin sticks and detonators, both of which are commonly used by real-estate contractors to blast hillocks. After the twin blasts in 2003, senior cop and encounter specialist Vijay Salaskar raided several such contractors in Thane. At that time, Salaskar and his team seized a huge quantity of illegally stored explosives. But it was later found that gelatin sticks had not been used in the 2006 train blasts.

Next, the investigators looked into when and where the bombs had been planted. After studying the design of the attack, they concluded that the planters got into the trains at Churchgate station and got off before Dadar station. This was the pre-CCTV era, when investigations, even those into the most common ones of train accidents and suicides, depended solely on eyewitness accounts. None of the bomb planters were intercepted at the railway station itself, hinting that the terrorists had literally melted into the crowd.

At hospital morgues, three days after the blasts, a few dead bodies remained unclaimed even though several families were still looking for their missing kin. Investigators and hospital authorities were being especially cautious after a victim's family wrote to the commissioner of police, A.N. Roy, saying that their father's body seemed to have been claimed by someone else. Their concern wasn't unfounded—they had searched for their father in every hospital, but in vain. Out of these, one body was of particular interest to the investigators. The mutilated body was of a man in his mid-forties. Even this body had claimants, a couple from Madhya Pradesh and another from rural Maharashtra. They had come in search of their missing sons, but the age, body type and other attributes of their sons did not match this body.

Before the investigators could probe further, Lashkar-e-Kahar (the army of wrath), a terrorist organization, took responsibility for the attacks. The group, in an email to news channels, claimed that sixteen mujahids had executed the blasts. They had also claimed responsibility for the Sankat Mochan temple blast in Varanasi earlier that year. But none of the investigations so far suggested their involvement in the train bombings. The police soon ruled out their involvement in the blasts.

As misses in the investigation piled up and pressure from senior officers increased, a team of officers in the ATS was closing in on a local. His conversations and movements seemed to be getting more and more suspicious.

6

Breakthrough

ATS Inspector Bhimdev Rathod could not get his mind off that one body, or whatever remained of it, in the morgue at Sion Hospital. The body remained unidentified, the post-mortem report branding the remains as 'Hindu', a victim of the explosion that tore through a first-class compartment of a Mumbai local as it sped towards Matunga. 'Maybe he's a drug addict or a migrant worker with no family,' Rathod thought out loud as he sipped on his milky chai. 'Or maybe he's one of the men who placed the bombs.'

Four days had passed since the blasts. Rain had lashed the tired city on all four days. Hospitals continued to be flooded with patients and harried relatives. The city was getting back on its feet, slowly and painfully.

A couple of years short of turning fifty, Rathod's decades in the force dulled in the face of this case, the biggest of his career. On the day of the blasts, Rathod had reported as senior police inspector of the Mumbai Central Railway Police, the station that officially recorded the Matunga blast. But the very next day, Rathod reported at the ATS office—he had been transferred by an order of the director general of police to aid investigations here. The case and this unidentified body consumed his thoughts.

After much debate, the investigators decided that a facial reconstruction of these remains was necessary. Orders from his superiors percolated down to Rathod and he rang up Dr M.E. Yeolekar, the dean of Sion Hospital. 'Can we do a facial reconstruction?' he asked.

Sion Hospital's forensic team swung into action as soon as the formal request was made. Facial reconstruction is an elaborate procedure. Associate Professor Dr Harish Pathak, who worked on the facial reconstruction, accessed the remains before him: a skull bone, a half frontal face with a cracked maxilla (jaw), broken cheekbones and a part of the ribs. A team of plastic surgeons, dental experts and anatomy artists got together, along with forensic experts, to reconstruct the face and give it human shape. His teeth were examined to determine his age. 'He was a paan or gutkha eater. His teeth were stained,' noted Pathak.

~

At the ATS office, Additional Commissioner of Police Jaijeet Singh summoned Rathod. When Rathod walked into Singh's room, he was already in an animated conversation with two other senior police officers—Inspector Sunil Deshmukh and Inspector Vasant Tajne. Tajne, who was attached to the Worli police station, an area in south Mumbai flanked by the iconic Haji Ali dargah on one side and the Siddhivinayak temple on the other, was called on special deputation to the ATS to investigate the serial train blasts. As the four of them sat down in Singh's cabin, he handed them a number from which several calls to a location near the Bihar and Nepal border had been intercepted. The number belonged to Mumtaz Chaudhary, an Arabic teacher based in Navi Mumbai. This was probably the first clue to help them make an arrest. The investigators were curious about whom Mumtaz was in touch with—there were as many as five calls every day to that particular number.

The next day, Rathod, Tajne and Deshmukh were back in Singh's office with the information they had gathered. The calls were traced to a person named Kamal Ansari in Bihar. He was arrested in 2002 in Delhi with an AK-47 rifle. Kamal wore several hats—he was a tailor, a driver, a vegetable vendor; he did everything to bring his family, his wife, mother and five children, out of the abject poverty they lived in. But Kamal had a terrible temper, which always gave him away.

Mumtaz was Kamal's brother-in-law. After the serial train blasts, Mumtaz was deeply suspicious of Kamal, who had visited the city just before the blasts and had hurriedly left on the day of the attack.

Police Inspector Sunil Deshmukh left for Navi Mumbai to get hold of Mumtaz. After the anticipated resistance and hesitation, Mumtaz was arrested on 20 July. He knew any reckless move could lead him into more trouble. Two days earlier, another team of policemen had left the city and were tracking down Kamal in Bihar.

Tajne and his men arrived in Patna on 19 July. They got in touch with the local police at the Kotwali police station, and the joint force headed to Basupatti, a village close to the Nepal border, known for being a hotbed of infiltration. Around 2 a.m., the police scanned the area near Kamal's house, keeping an eye out for the slightest movement. Kamal was out of town, but was expected to be back by 3 a.m. He would cross the landmark Prasad Cinema in the village market on his way home. They didn't want to get too close to the house lest they alerted its residents, so they decided to apprehend him near Prasad Cinema itself. Six policemen, dressed like local villagers surrounded their target. As they saw Kamal approaching with a friend, they circled them and ordered them to surrender. But the Mumbai Police had underestimated Kamal.

Standing 6 feet tall, the man, dressed in a bright blue shirt and cream pants, towered above all of them, his rustic features giving him the appearance of a local movie star. He shoved the policemen aside and ran, but the chase was a short one and he found himself pinned down by the men soon enough. At the police station, he identified himself as Kamal Ahmed Ansari, a toy seller. The friend accompanying Kamal was baffled by everything that was unfolding around him. It was a perfectly normal day for Khalid Shaikh before he found himself being arrested for a crime he didn't even know had occurred. He was so stunned that he didn't even put up a fight before his arrest.

Meanwhile, the police seized a Nokia mobile phone from Kamal and decided to conduct a thorough search of his house. As police vehicles whizzed through the village, its inhabitants watched in rapt attention. The police pulled Kamal out of their vehicle by his collar. Kamal's wife, Tabassum Sultana, dressed modestly in a salwar kameez with a dupatta on her head, opened the door. The team searched his decrepit two-storey home for clues. One of the police officers pulled out a polythene bag neatly hidden below the wooden cot. It contained a black powder that Kamal insisted was detergent gone bad. But the powder smelled nothing like detergent. Tajne seized the contents of the packet, among other things. A small portion was separated for testing.

The police teams then scanned the first floor of the house, which didn't yield much. But the ATS had made its first big arrest. The team took a flight back to Mumbai with both arrested men, Kamal and his friend Khalid Shaikh. Tajne wanted to be extra cautious about the powder they had seized, so a policeman was sent in a train, as taking the powder by air could be dangerous.

As Kamal's questioning began, more information started pouring in. On 23 July, Rathod went to the Crime Branch Unit II office near Jacob Circle to take Tanveer into custody. The Crime Branch, which was simultaneously conducting investigations into the case, had arrested him from the M.H. Saboo Siddique Maternity and General Hospital, where he worked as a medical registrar. Rathod brought Tanveer to the ATS office and began his interrogation.

Over the next few days, the Crime Branch managed to get hold of four more suspects, all SIMI activists—Suhail and Zameer, brothers Faisal and Muzzammil. It was Faisal's arrest that turned the fortunes of the investigators.

He was the brain behind the blasts.

With eight accused in custody, the ATS officers wondered if they were on the right track. But they needed a concrete headway in the case. Rathod decided to search Tanveer's house to get more leads. He left with Tanveer for Agripada's BIT chawl. The entire house was searched as Tanveer's elderly father stared at the police wide-eyed. But nothing suspicious was found.

On his way back, Rathod inquired about Tanveer's passport. It was with International Trade Links, a travel agency in Fort, Mumbai. Rathod went to the travel agency office and asked the manager, Krishna Pillai, if he could identify Tanveer. 'Yes, he had submitted his passport for a visa a few months ago,' said the manager. As Rathod scanned through the passport, he found a visa for Iran.

The next house searched belonged to Faisal, at Bandra's Perry Cross Road. This apartment, where the first meeting to plan the serial blasts had taken place, was opened using a spare key that Faisal had hidden above the door. During the search, the police found a clothes rack made of fabric, a zip running down its length; the fabric was stained by a black, powdery substance. The powder was carefully wiped off the rack with cotton and collected in a plastic bag. In another small pouch, the police found return railway tickets to Howrah in West Bengal, ICICI Bank debit cards, a diving licence issued by the Pune Regional Transport Office (RTO) and thirty-two Saudi riyals, documents of a Bajaj Pulsar motorcycle and a rent agreement for the flat. The police also seized SIMI literature—one of the books was titled *Atankwad ka Zimmedar Kaun?* (Who's Responsible for Terrorism?)—along with maps of Mumbai city and its suburbs, and maps of Pakistan, Iran, Muscat, Afghanistan and Tehran, among others. On the Mumbai maps, some places were marked with red and green ink. A route traversing Mumbai–Tehran–Zahidan–Muzaffarabad was marked out on one of the maps.

The police were baffled by the Iran link. This was the second time they found a mention of Iran and a trip to the border areas of the country. Iran is a Shia country, with no track record of hostility against India. On the other hand, all the accused were Sunni Muslims. Iran had never been used as a launch pad for terror activities against India, even by the most radical terrorists. It was confusing to try and decipher this new link.

Other details found were an international mobile number, an email ID (guddu_sir@yahoo.com) and an Airtel SIM card.

The next search carried out was in Muzzammil's house in Tirupati Apartment, Mira Road.

In the second-floor flat, the police found a disconnected CPU on a computer trolley. In the next room, they found two more brand-new CPUs, still packed in cardboard boxes. In another bag, they found a CD with the name Rahil Shaikh written on it.

The search also yielded a graduation certificate for a BSc (IT) degree from Bhartiya Shiksha Parishad in Uttar Pradesh, an appointment letter from Data Core Technology, an identity card from Oracle, SIMI literature and the same book that was found in Faisal's house, along with the same maps. However, Muzzammil's and Rahil's degree certificates turned out to be fake. A separate case was registered against them for these fake certificates.

In the meantime, the Iran link continued to flummox the police. In desperation, they began a crackdown on travel agents organizing tours to Iran. Over 200 travel agents were hauled to the ATS office and their statements recorded by the police. They found that every year, lakhs of Indians visit Iran to pay their respects at the holy shrines in Mashhad and Qom. But the people who visited these shrines were all Shia Muslims.

The most important clue the police discovered was that all the pilgrims considered it to be a privilege to partake of the sacred food served at the shrine of Imam Reza in Mashhad and got a sticker endorsed on the back page of their passports as evidence of their visit to the shrine. This whole process was an expression of religious devotion. But all the accused who had gone to Iran did not have similar stickers on their passports, indicating that they had given the shrine a miss.

For the ATS, it was an education in the religious practices of the two major Muslim sects. They realized that the radicalized men used the Iran visit only as a ruse to throw investigators off-track while they actually travelled to Pakistan via Tehran. After landing in Tehran, they just crossed over from Sistan to Pakistan, and came back using the same route, instead of heading to Mashhad or Qom, to avoid any suspicion.

The interrogations revealed that Faisal and Muzzammil were in touch with the LeT commander Azam Cheema through Rahil and Dawrey, who now lived in Jeddah. Rahil and Rizwan routed the money from Cheema to Faisal. Faisal, in turn, used the money to prepare for the mission and got a few like-minded people to train in Pakistan. Thus, Rahil, Dawrey and Cheema became the most wanted accused in the case. Further interrogations of the duo in October led the sleuths to a marshy land near the Dahisar subway along the railway tracks. Near an electrical cabin numbered L-16, they pointed to a brown plastic bag, half submerged in the mud. The police got their hands and feet dirty as they attempted to pull the bag out. Inside, they found seven rubber rings, the kind that is used inside a pressure cooker, and five stainless-steel whistles used in pressure cookers—all of them bore the brand name Kanchan. There were other articles, like red and white insulation wires, two clamps and a black wire with a Nokia switch. For a long time, the police had tossed around the theory of the bombs being kept in pressure cookers. With this new-found evidence, their theory was turning out to be credible. It was just a matter of recording the confessions and putting across the evidence in front of a court.

On 28 July, Ehtesham Siddiqui was arrested by the ATS for publishing inflammatory SIMI literature. This was the time SIMI members—both current and retired—were being rounded up for interrogation. They were asked to report every few days. During one such session, Ehtesham revealed that Tanveer was going to teach him how to make liquid bombs. Rathod realized Tanveer was revealing information to the police only in bits and pieces. Investigators, at that point, knew nothing about these liquid bombs Ehtesham had mentioned. Rathod's next move was to grill Tanveer on this new revelation.

It was August and almost twenty days had passed since the serial train blasts. Rathod was restless, the arrested accused were tougher than he had thought they would be. Many of them had trained in Pakistan and they reflected an uncanny grit. As these thoughts clouded his mind, a message arrived from Tanveer, who was in the lock-up. He wanted to make a statement. Rathod did not waste a minute and rushed to the dimly lit interrogation room. Tanveer sat on a wooden chair, looking tense. 'I will tell you everything. *Main aapko sab batata hoon,*' Tanveer said. 'I have hidden everything at my brother's house.'

A police team, headed by Rathod, immediately left for Saat Rasta, close to the iconic Mahalaxmi temple. Tanveer guided them to room no. 31 in BIT chawl. Tanveer's mother opened the door, and, on his insistence, let the police into his brother's house in the neighbouring building called Pila Mahal with the only pair of keys in her possession. Seeing Tanveer in handcuffs, his mother could not hold back her tears. As the police entered the second-floor house in Pila Mahal, Tanveer's handcuffs were opened. He led them to a cupboard that contained maps, locations of training camps and SIMI literature. They also found the same book: *Atankwad ka Zimmedar Kaun?* Unlike in the other searches, the police did not find any powder that they suspected to be explosives. Tanveer also spilt the beans about his and Ehtesham Siddiqui's role in the mission; the latter was already in the ATS's custody. But the police were reluctant to trust Tanveer. He was shrewd and every time they interrogated him, he revealed information in bits and pieces, which kept investigators occupied for days. Rathod felt that Tanveer could have been wasting their time. But they went along with what he said. On 12 August, when Rathod and Inspector Wardhankar interrogated Tanveer one more time, he agreed to hand over the chemicals that could be used to make bombs. He directed the police to the M.H. Saboo Siddique Hospital, where he claimed to have hidden the 'explosives'. The police promptly drove him through the narrow lanes of Bhendi Bazaar, a Muslim-dominated area, to the hospital. For his identification, they lifted Tanveer's veil and let the staff identify him. He guided them to a small room next to the Intensive Care Unit (ICU) from where he pulled out three bottles full of liquids that looked like chemicals. Tanveer said the bottles contained hydrogen peroxide, acetone and sulphuric acid, all of which can be used to make liquid bombs. The police sent the chemicals for testing. Tanveer also told the police that his brother, Ishtiaq Ansari, had the mobile phone that was used during the blasts for communication. It was seized.

~

It was two months since the blasts and the investigators continued following the same trail. Locals were being thoroughly interrogated and called in frequently for questioning. Meanwhile, every accused led them to the maps, some leftover electrical components and a lot of unanswered questions about how the mission was planned and executed. On 29 September, Sajid Marghoob Ansari, who worked in Mumbai's Malwani area, was arrested, along with three others—Naved Hussain Khan, Mohammed Ali Alam Shaikh and Abdul Wahideen Mohammad Shaikh.

While Naved was arrested from Hyderabad, Abdul Wahid, an assistant schoolteacher, who was a regular at the

ATS office in view of the crackdown, was called to the local police station as well and arrested. Sajid juggled running a mobile and computer hardware repair shop with teaching teens the same skill set.

Mohammed Ali Alam Shaikh was arrested by the Borivali Railway Police from Govandi, a central part of the city that mostly consists of slums. A search of his house on plot no. 33 in the slum cluster yielded something substantial for the police. The two-storey structure was like any other cluttered house. A storage bed that took up most of the space in the house contained old clothes, other unwanted household articles and a pressure cooker with its brand name shining bright—Kanchan. The police wondered why a pressure cooker was packed inside the bed. On the inside of the bed, they saw a few black and white spots. The police wiped off the spots with cotton and collected it as samples in a plastic bag. They also searched the upper section of the house, where Mohammed Ali's brother lived with his wife.

The next day, another team led by Inspector Deshmukh left for Malwani to search the office of Sajid, a resident of Mira Road. This search yielded one soldering gun, four pieces of soldering wires, soldering paste, a screwdriver, two stainless-steel tweezers, a multimeter, a packet of Airtel recharge vouchers with a sticker stating the SIM and mobile number, and a few other electric components like resistors, capacitors, coils, transistors, LEDs, diodes, etc., dumped in a plastic bag that had the name Priya Gold, a biscuit brand, stamped on it. The investigators concluded that while most of these items were likely to be used in Sajid's day job, they could also be used to assemble bombs.

During the questioning, there was one person every SIMI member was asked about—Asif Bashir Khan from Jalgaon.

He had been declared a proclaimed offender in a case involving two Jalgaon locals, who were sent to Kashmir. Investigators from the ATS were becoming more anxious with each passing day—he had evaded arrest for far too long. Finally, on 2 October, Tajne headed to interrogate Asif, after a tip-off. Asif, suspected of being one of the planters, was arrested in Belgaum, and driven to his temporary accommodation in Poonam Park apartments in Mira Road. Asif directed them to room no. 101, his house, in the building. When the police nudged him to open the door, Asif claimed that he had lost the keys. A key maker was called and the door was opened. In the bedroom, the police laid their hands on a black Rexine bag. Inside a plastic pouch, they found white granules that had a strong smell. Samples of these granules were sent for testing. Another small bag inside the Rexine bag contained ten aluminium tubes, with wires placed inside plastic bottles. They were electronic detonators. In another room, the police found twenty-three books in Urdu and two files with several documents piled inside them. Asif was later also identified as the tenant of that flat by the building's chairman and secretary.

On 20 October, the court directed ATS officers to destroy the ten live detonators found in possession of one of the accused. Tajne appointed Sub-inspector Sandesh Revle from the Bomb Detection and Disposal Squad to carry out the task. Revle and his men drove with the detonators to Girgaum Chowpatty, a beach in south Mumbai. Carefully, each detonator was taken out of the vehicle and placed in a drill hole along with the explosives, in the sand. The holes were covered with sand and an additional sandbag was used to secure them. After cordoning off the area—it is a popular tourist and local hang-out—Revle and Tajne watched ten blasts as their men set off the detonators one after the other. The impact was such that the heavy sandbag too flew up in the air. With every thud, the sleuths imagined the impact of the blast in the compartments of the local trains. Revle shuddered, shaking his head to dismiss the thought. The perpetrators need to be taught a lesson, Revle thought, almost angered by the sight of the blasts in the sand. He walked towards the pits and called for his men. One by one, they collected all the debris from the sand blasts—picking up the remains of the detonators, wires and castings, the same way the city was left to fend for itself three months ago.

7

The Pakistani Mercenary—An Encounter

22 August 2006

It was 4.15 a.m. Two vehicles with half a dozen policemen were headed towards a rundown building in Antop Hill's sector number seven. They had to complete their mission before sunrise. As the vehicles stopped near the building, the men got down and pulled out a man in his twenties from one of the cars. Shivering, the man said in a hushed voice, '*Sahab, yahi jagah hai. Idhar hi milne ko bola tha. Woh upar teen maale pe hoga.* (Sir, this is the place. We were going to meet here. He must be on the third floor.)' Inspector Sunil Deshmukh signalled his team to take the man back to the ATS office while he waited there and calculated his next move. The man was referring to a Pakistani national.

~

A day earlier, Deshmukh had been on the trail of a blue Maruti car that was possibly doing a reconnaissance in Mumbai. The

ATS team was working on the information from an alert sent by central agencies that a few Pakistanis involved in the 7/11 blasts were still in Mumbai and were planning another terror strike. This time it would be during the Ganesh Utsav, an eleven-day festival celebrating the elephant-headed Hindu deity, Ganesha. The festival, one of the biggest for the city as well as the state, was just eight days away. Deshmukh hoped that tracking these men would not only avert a disaster, but also hold the key to the investigation in the 7/11 train blasts.

The police had no information about the location of the terrorists; they could be anywhere—in a slum, a high-rise or in an under-construction building. The only clue was a Maruti car with a Gujarat state number plate. The search for the car had to be a secret and was limited to Deshmukh, his team and their network. These precautions were to keep both corrupt police officers and the media at bay. Soon the car was located; it was moving near Sion. Deshmukh and his team decided to follow the vehicle before arresting its driver. He also decided not to take the help of the police wireless network or block any of the city roads by deploying *nakabandi* (blockades put up by the police). One mistake could ruin everything. The team followed the car right up to Wadala through Antop Hill and Sion. At one point, the driver of the vehicle being tailed was so rash that Deshmukh thought he might be aware of their presence. The chase intensified as the driver now attempted to speed away from the police. Eventually, the police vehicle overtook the Maruti car and forced it to a screeching halt. A man wearing a Pathani suit jumped out and began to run, but the constables, who had jumped out of the police jeep, pinned him down immediately. He was brought in front of Deshmukh, who questioned him about his identity. The man refused to reveal his name at first, but later told the police that he was Riyaz Nawabuddin from Pakistan.

The constables frantically searched the Maruti car and found a black bag, with one Star pistol, five rounds of ammunition, 1520 grams of RDX, four railway tickets, five detonators and some US dollars on the passenger seat. They also found multiple number plates in the car, which meant that the vehicle could be a stolen one. But the quantity of the explosives seized was just 1.5 kilograms, which made Deshmukh suspicious. He thought the terrorists could possibly be on a dry run to carry out a blast and, thus, were not carrying many explosives to avoid suspicion.

Nawabuddin was taken to the interrogation room in the ATS headquarters in Nagpada. Soon after Deshmukh entered the room, he noticed Nawabuddin shudder, as droplets of sweat trickled down his temple. There was pin-drop silence in the room before Deshmukh screamed at the top of his voice demanding an explanation for the explosives found in his car. At first, Nawabuddin said that they did not belong to him. He narrated a cock-and-bull story about how he was jobless and had come to Mumbai looking for work. But Deshmukh was in no mood for stories. He slapped Nawabuddin so hard that he fell off the chair. Two constables rushed forward, picked him up and made him sit in the chair again. For the next half hour, Nawabuddin sang like a canary, bombarding the investigators with information. It was now for them to sieve the truth.

Nawabuddin confessed to Deshmukh that he was a Pakistani national and had sneaked into India six–seven months ago through the guarded yet porous India–Pakistan border. After entering India through Kashmir, he went to Delhi, and then headed to Uttaranchal. He promised an unsuspecting youngster a job in the Gulf, took the necessary documents and used this man's identity for a job in an industrial estate in Dehradun. He had come to Mumbai only four days ago and was awaiting further instructions from his handlers in Pakistan.

Nawabuddin was trained in handling weapons and making bombs in PoK, where he worked as an autorickshaw driver, until he came in contact with a terror outfit. He was promised a handsome price and a good life if he agreed to help carry out an attack on India, against the kafirs (Muslims who had stayed back in India after Partition). This was his first assignment and he was sent to Mumbai to join his counterparts who had already made their way into the city. He was told that the explosives and the money would be delivered to him, but wasn't told anything else, including where to go in Mumbai. A phone call from Pakistan four days ago clarified that an associate would get in touch with him soon. 'Sit tight until you receive further instructions,' he was told by one of the handlers.

Nawabuddin confessed that, since his arrival in Mumbai, he had been living with a friend, Mohammad Ali alias Abu Umed alias Abu Osama, in an abandoned building in Antop Hill and had been on his way to a friend's place with the explosives. Nawabuddin had no choice but to agree to show the police his hideout. He explained that the dilapidated Antop Hill building was chosen as the safe house because it was secluded and mostly empty. Abu Umed and Nawabuddin lived on the third floor, in a one-bedroom house. The flat had an unbroken door, but the rest of the building was in disrepair and none of the other flats had doors or windows. The police asked Nawabuddin to point out the building as they neared the area where they believed Abu Umed was hiding.

When Deshmukh asked Nawabuddin for information on his handlers and the train blasts, he claimed to have no knowledge. He, however, revealed that Abu Umed had been living in Mumbai for much longer and that he might know more. Nawabuddin described his accomplice as a quiet man. Whenever Nawabuddin asked him any questions about their plan in Mumbai, he would tell him to wait for the right time. Nawabuddin said that Abu Umed came home very late at night, mostly in the wee hours.

Wide-eyed that entire night, Deshmukh had a hunch that this was a good lead. It was now his responsibility to make the most of it.

~

Around 3.30 a.m., a police constable woke Nawabuddin up. He splashed water on his face and tried to wake up. The constable dragged him into a jeep and headed towards Antop Hill, based on his directions. He sat in the jeep with three policemen, including Deshmukh. Three other officers, Inspector Vasant Tajne, Sub-inspector Sachin Kadam and Sub-inspector Kandalkar, followed in a second jeep. As the police cars sped towards Antop Hill, Nawabuddin pleaded to be spared. Deshmukh pushed him away and warned him to remain quiet; he had far more important things on his mind at that moment. Both the vehicles came to a halt after Nawabuddin pointed towards the building. It was a fully constructed structure that had remained empty for some reason. The signboard at the gate of the building said 'CHS'.

Deshmukh jumped out of the car with Tajne and the other officers, who pulled out Nawabuddin. '*Pakka yahi hai?* (You are sure this is the building?)' asked Deshmukh. '*Haan, sahab. Yahi hai. Woh upar teen maale pe rehta hai.* (Yes, sir. This is the one. He lives on the third floor).'

It was pitch-dark outside and the desolate building looked eerie. Deshmukh's mind raced. They had to arrest Abu Umed alive. He could prove to be a treasure trove of information. Armed with revolvers, the three senior officers and three constables decided to enter the building. One ATS officer had already taken Nawabuddin back to the office. Slowly and cautiously, the police began to make their way up the creaking stairway. The darkness confused the police. Had someone been watching them all this while? The lights on the third floor were switched off; the absence of windows ensured the surrounding remained pitch-dark. When the police tried the door, it was locked from inside. The target was home. The men first tried to check if they could enter through another way, but there wasn't one. So they took their positions and began closing in on the door. They tried to pick up on any movement or voices on the inside. They heard nothing but the chirping of crickets in the night's deadly silence.

Deshmukh went ahead and knocked on the door. There was no response. Identifying themselves as cops, they knocked again and asked Abu Umed to surrender. There was still no response from the other side. Suddenly, a thud startled the police. A bullet had flown out from the closed door and had hit a pillar in front of the house. Within seconds, another bullet was fired from inside. Abu Umed seemed to be following the instruction that he shouldn't be arrested at any cost. He was equipped with an AK-47, a fierce weapon compared to the police revolvers. But it was one man against six. The police rained bullets until the firing from inside ceased. Deshmukh carefully broke open the door, or whatever was left of it. He was at risk of being killed if Abu Umed had been playing the police by deliberately stopping the firing. Inside, Abu Umed lay still in a pool of blood. Deshmukh bent down to check his pulse; there was no sign of life. He promptly informed the control room at 6 a.m. that their mission had ended.

Deshmukh, along with the other policemen, looked for evidence inside Abu Umed's room. The room had been cleaned, dusted and washed, and all his belongings were neatly arranged. They were surprised at how organized the room was, indicating the discipline with which Abu Umed worked. There was a bed sheet spread on the ground with a backpack taking the place of a pillow. A pile of clothes was stashed there too. When the police checked his bag, they found dry clothes, three loaded magazines with seventy-two rounds of ammunition, nine-volt batteries, a green plastic tin, white powder, 13 to 15 grams of RDX, $50, a telephone diary and three maps—a world map, a map of Maharashtra and one of Mumbai. The map of Mumbai had four spots marked on it—Byculla and Bandra railway stations, Siddhivinayak temple and Anushakti Nagar, where the Bhabha Atomic and Research Centre, a premier multidisciplinary nuclear research centre, is located.

Abu Umed's body had seven bullet injuries on it, all on the torso. The objects recovered from his room showed that he was trained in making bombs and was possibly in the process of making one. In a matter of minutes he had fired eighteen rounds at the police, while the police had retaliated by firing twenty-one rounds during the shootout. The investigators sent his body for a post-mortem and the area was cordoned off for a *panchnama*.

This was the only shoot-out in the city soon after the train blasts in July. Investigators were now trying to ascertain if Nawabuddin had any links with the Jaish-e-Mohammed terrorists, Mohammad Zubair and Mohammed Sohail, who were arrested by the Border Security Force in Kolkata on 12 August, while trying to cross the Ichamati River by boat. Zubair had told the investigators that he had to meet a person in Sealdah to collect air tickets to go to Mumbai. The investigators also needed evidence to reveal Abu Umed's true identity.

Faisal, who was already being interrogated, had told the police that all the twelve people trained in operating firearms and ammunition had sneaked into the country through the Bangladesh, Nepal and Kutch borders. Nawabuddin said the same thing about Abu Umed.

Deshmukh's and Tajne's investigations also suggested that a local helped Abu Umed and Nawabuddin find the Antop Hill flat. A few residents nearby claimed they had often seen an Indica car parked at the gate of the abandoned building. Who could this local be?

~

Though investigators claimed that Abu Umed was one of the Pakistanis who helped the bomb planters in the 7/11 blasts, they managed to produce little evidence justifying this claim. The mystery of these Pakistani men gave the police many sleepless nights as questions were raised about the authenticity of the encounter. In the end, the police failed to get evidence beyond reproof against Abu Umed.

Soon after the encounter, Nawabuddin was booked for the possession of the arms and ammunition he was caught with, and was sentenced to five years in jail. After his release in 2011, ATS sleuths deported him to Pakistan by taking him right up to Attari station at the Wagah border and seating him in a train to Pakistan. After that day, no one ever heard about him.

But why wasn't he cited as a witness in the 7/11 train blasts case and why wasn't he used as an incontrovertible piece of walking evidence against the neighbours whom India always considers to be at the root of all its problems?

It's a mystery that remains unsolved.

8

The Suicide Mystery

26 August 2006

A month had passed since the serial train blasts. By now, nine people had been arrested by the ATS, but the case was far from closed. The long list of accused were still free baffled the police; the terror puzzle was becoming messier each day.

It was a Saturday. Assistant Commissioner of Police (ACP) Vinod Bhat was extremely restless. His desk was piled high with papers, all related to the train blasts case. He had scoured through the statements and panchnamas, and examined the evidence gathered to prepare a report. But Bhat couldn't figure out what to make out of the entire investigation. Something bothered him. A presidential award–winning fifty-four-year-old officer, Bhat was an expert in paperwork. His reports were highly appreciated among the top brass in the police. But he remained distracted by something. He had tried to talk to several colleagues, but no one had the time or the patience to listen. Bhat was appointed to supervise the 7/11 investigations along with another ACP, Yashwant

Tawde. Since the blasts, Tawde too had burnt the midnight oil putting pieces of information together to get to the real story behind the blasts.

That day, at noon, Bhat called his orderly. He asked him to bring Ehtesham Siddiqui, one of the accused and an office-bearer of SIMI, to his cabin. Ehtesham, accused of planting a bomb in one of the seven trains, had given a statement to the investigators. Bhat wanted to confirm his statement. Within the next five minutes, two policemen stood in Bhat's cabin holding Ehtesham. Bhat gestured the policemen to leave. He offered Ehtesham a glass of water and asked him to speak up. 'Daro mat, sach batao (Don't be scared, tell the truth),' Bhat told Ehtesham, who began to narrate his story. He told Bhat about how he was picked up by the Kurla police in September 2001, along with eight others, and arrested for being a part of a banned terror outfit (SIMI) under the Unlawful Activities (Prevention) Act (UAPA) 1967. 'They told me that the Students Islamic Movement of India has been declared as a banned organization. The court released me on bail, but the Kurla police, instead of releasing me, took me to the police station and put me inside the lock-up again. They framed me in false cases and have spoiled my reputation in society,' Ehtesham told Bhat, adding that he had to give up his engineering course due to this. He also told Bhat about his publishing house, through which he published Islamic literature, and how, despite his qualifications, the arrest and false implication in the 11 July 2006 Mumbai serial train blasts case had destroyed his career.

'On the evening of 11 July 2006, I was at home. When I learnt about the blast in Mira Road, I went to the blast site to help the victims. I knew very well I would eventually be detained by the local police for a formal inquiry. It has been this way since 2001. A senior police inspector, named Murade, of Mira Road police station, came to my house on the evening of 13 July 2006 and asked me to come to the police station the next day. On 14 July 2006 at 11 a.m., I went to the Mira Road police station again to meet Murade. He questioned me about my whereabouts and asked me for my phone number, which I gave him willingly. He told me that if required, I would be called for further investigation,' Ehtesham recalled. He added that a cop visited him again on 24 July and asked him to come to the ATS office in Nagpada. 'They took me to Bhoiwada and put me in a lock-up, and began beating me with belts and sticks and continued beating me till the evening. Later, they took me from Bhoiwada to Nagpada, handcuffed,' he said. Bhat offered him another glass of water and assured Ehtesham that if he was indeed innocent, no one could implicate him in any case. He was then sent back to the lock-up.

Two days later, on 28 August, Bhat was running late to work; he reported to the Bhoiwada ATS office at 10.30 a.m., forty-five minutes later than usual. As the tall, fair, bespectacled man walked through the corridors, junior officers in his office promptly stood up to greet him. But Bhat did not look up at anyone, just nodded and walked ahead. His colleagues were surprised to see him walk past without greeting them. A genial man with a pleasant disposition, it was uncharacteristic of him to pass by without talking to anyone. That day, he walked straight into his cabin, but did not look at any files. A chain-smoker, he kept lighting one cigarette after another. At lunch, his food remained untouched. He was finally interrupted, at 4 p.m., by his deputy, who informed him about a meeting at the Western Railway control room.

The meeting, scheduled for 4.30 p.m., was attended by Bhat, fifteen officers from the ATS and the deputy commissioner of police, Nawal Bajaj. The meeting attempted to recreate the sequence of events on 11 July. Bhat remained distracted and did not speak at the meeting. At 6.30 p.m., the officers returned to the ATS office in Bhoiwada and half an hour later, Bhat's driver picked him up from the office. On his way home, Bhat asked the driver to take him to Siddhivinayak temple. As soon as they reached the temple, Bhat got down from the car and asked the driver to go home. The driver was surprised that he was not asked to wait, but he refrained from questioning his employer, and quietly drove back to Bhat's home.

ACP Tawde, who was part of the team investigating the bomb blasts, received a call around 10 p.m. A GRP officer from Dadar informed him about an accident on the railway tracks. The victim had been rushed to Sion Hospital. Tawde and other officers hurried to the hospital, where they were handed over a blood-soaked identity card, a pack of 555 cigarettes and a ten-rupee note. The GRP officials reported that motorman Virendra Singh, manning a train headed to CST, in south Mumbai, had noticed a man crossing the tracks at 9.22 p.m. The person was so close that Singh was unable to stop the train in time to save him. The man was knocked down by his train below the Tilak bridge, barely 100 metres away from platform no. 3. Under the stationmaster's supervision the victim was immediately rushed to Sion Hospital, where he was declared dead. The man now lying in the hospital was identified as ACP Vinod Bhat.

Bhat, an officer from the 1972–74 batch, was known for his lectures on the Maharashtra Control of Organised Crime Act (MCOCA) and Terrorist and Disruptive Activities (Prevention) Act (TADA) in the Maharashtra Police Academy, where he had previously been a deputy director. He had been honoured three times by the President, with the gallantry award, the Sword of Honour and the President's medal, during his thirty-two-year career in the force. Known to be an upright officer, he was held in high esteem by his colleagues. He was temporarily shifted to the ATS after the train blasts and was assigned to handle the paperwork of the case, which included compiling statements, evidence and preparing charges. He also personally interrogated the men accused of the blasts.

His death shocked the city police. But the mystery surrounding his death set tongues wagging. Was it an accident or did he kill himself? What was he doing near the railway tracks when he never took a train? Was he under too much pressure with regard to the 7/11 investigations? Or was it the pressures of his personal life? A lawyer close to Bhat had told the investigators that he was under 'tremendous pressure' due to the blasts, while another officer pointed out that Bhat was concerned about the case registered against his wife, Seema.

A member of a police housing scheme, Seema was dealing with allegations concerning a property dispute. In the first week of August, a First Information Report (FIR) was lodged against fourteen people, including Seema, at the Santacruz police station. One person had been arrested and more arrests were likely. Bhat could have been worried about his wife.

Bhat's death did not affect the blast investigations. As days passed, his memory began to fade from the minds of his peers. However, a curious twist during the trial of the men accused in the 7/11 blasts brought back unpleasant memories of Bhat's death.

Ehtesham entered the witness box on 30 April 2013. In his testimony, he told the court that Bhat killed himself because of pressure from his seniors to 'implicate' young men in the case.

'I was taken back to Bhoiwada lock-up on the night of 24 August 2006. I was taken to the second floor two days after that and presented before ACP Vinod Bhat. He inquired about the case and told me that he had read all the paperwork and that he was sure that the other persons and I, who had been arrested till then, were not involved in the bomb blasts. He told me that there is tremendous pressure on him from [then commissioner of police] A.N. Roy and [ATS chief] K.P. Raghuvanshi to prepare and file a false case against us in connection with the blasts. He told me that he is not ready to act as per their say, but they were pressurizing him, saying that they would involve his wife in a case. I was then sent back to my lock-up. He said that he would give up his life, but not involve us in the false case. Some days thereafter, a constable was reading a newspaper outside the lock-up and I happened to read the title of a news item saying that ACP Vinod Bhat had committed suicide.'

Raghuvanshi, however, rubbished all rumours of Bhat being under pressure of seniors who were 'implicating men' in the 7/11 blasts. They said that Bhat had played no direct role in the investigations and his job was restricted only to analysing documents.

Bhat's death went down in police files as an 'accident due to trespassing'. The truth will always remain shrouded in mystery and perhaps Bhat took the secret of his death to the grave.

9

A Soldier from Pakistan

On a wet September morning, Inspector Iqbal Shaikh was seated in his makeshift office in Bhoiwada, studying the backlog of cases since the blasts, when the sound of footsteps distracted him. The 7/11 blast investigations were so intense that ATS officers had converted the area around the lock-ups into their workspace, filled with desks, chairs and files. Shaikh had looked at the accused in the lock-up before walking up to his desk on the first floor. He was sifting through papers when his deputy had walked in. 'Sir, Hashmi is creating a ruckus. He wants to talk to you.' Thirty-five-year-old Tafheem Akmal Hashmi, an accused in the 7/11 train blasts, was kept in a lock-up on the ground floor of the ATS office. A resident of Perozshah in Pakistan, Hashmi was arrested by the Indian Army in Gulabgadh in Kashmir.

Hashmi, who limped and was also nursing a fractured arm, walked into Shaikh's cabin looking tormented. He broke down as soon as he saw Shaikh. '*Sahab, woh mujhe maar dega. Usne dhamki di hai* (Sir, he will kill me. He has threatened me.).' Shaikh calmed him down and asked him who he was referring to. Hashmi's reply surprised Shaikh. 'Sahab, Faisal,' he said, almost shivering with fear. Given Hashmi's strong build and icy-cold demeanour, it was difficult to picture anyone threatening him. Shaikh wondered why Faisal would want to kill Hashmi.

Hashmi's parents, originally from Kashmir, had crossed over to Pakistan after Partition. He blamed Hindus for killing his grandfather, who died while crossing the border. Such incidents sowed the seeds of hatred against India in him. Schooled in a village, he graduated with a BSc degree from a college in the Gujarat district of Pakistan. A rebel, Hashmi joined the Pakistan Army in the 1990s soon after he completed his studies. His first posting was that of *hawaldar* and he was subsequently posted in the 637 Infantry, in Bhinder, PoK. After he left the army, he came in contact with terrorists, who encouraged him to join them. Soon, he began to train in the hills of Afghanistan and PoK, followed by a three-year training camp in Muzaffarabad, where he learnt to use arms and ammunitions. In 1997, Hashmi returned to Kashmir and asked his aunt's son whether he could rejoin the force. His cousin Sayeed Mazhar was a lieutenant colonel in the unit that Hashmi joined. Hashmi was posted in the 637 Infantry in Bhinder again, but he soon quit to join the terrorist organization Al-Badr (The Full Moon), run by Jasniel Rihal in the Jammu and Kashmir region. The group was allegedly formed by Pakistan's ISI in June 1998 and is believed to be operating independently from their previous affiliate, Hizb-ul-Mujahideen.

At the time of his arrest, Hashmi was a divisional commander in the terror outfit, posted in Jammu and Udhampur. He was arrested by Indian troops from the Nandmarg forest near Shopian in south Kashmir on 23 August 2006. When the ATS sought his custody in the train blasts case a few days later,

Hashmi was languishing in a jail in Srinagar. A popular Hindi news channel had telecast a video in which he claimed to know about the 7/11 blasts and its perpetrators. For the ATS, Hashmi was a welcome lead who could possibly provide a link between those already arrested and those still on the run.

Hashmi was brought to the ATS office in Mumbai on 2 September 2006, where he was arrested for the train blasts. He remained in custody for a month, during which he sent this message to Shaikh.

Shaikh was puzzled by Hashmi's claim and asked for more details. Hashmi told him that he had met Faisal during a training camp in Muzaffarabad. Hashmi's Al-Badr training camp was just a little further down from the camp where Faisal had received his training. On one occasion, Faisal had stopped by the Al-Badr camp and approached Hashmi for a glass of water. Hashmi offered him Rooh Afza and they had a brief conversation. During their brief conversation, Hashmi was pleased to know that Faisal was from Mumbai and was headed to become a mujahid, just like him. Despite his hatred for the country, the city of Mumbai had always fascinated Hashmi. He had wished Faisal luck and the two of them had parted ways. That was the only time the two had spoken before their arrest.

Hashmi's statement was crucial to establish that Faisal was an LeT operative. Shaikh rushed to his superiors and they called a meeting. Hashmi's statement was recorded before a judicial magistrate, under section 164 of the Criminal Procedure Code, so that it would be of greater value in a court as compared to a statement recorded by a police officer. The police failed to find any evidence indicating that Hashmi was involved in the 7/11 blasts, but he was still an important witness to prove Faisal's presence in the training camps in Muzaffarabad. Hashmi's statement was formally recorded on 13 October 2006, and he was discharged from the 7/11 case at the time of the filing of the charge sheet in November. After he was discharged, he was sent back to the jail in Srinagar, from where he had been brought. He was cited as a prime witness instead.

~

Seven years later, a bearded Hashmi stood confidently in the witness box, dressed in a Pathani suit. During this final testimony in court, he was declared a hostile witness as he relayed nothing that was recorded in his earlier statement. He accused army officers of tutoring him before he appeared on television to declare that he knew about the 7/11 blasts.

'I made the statement on television in the army camp area. The statement was based on the instructions of the army people [to say] that the Lashkar is behind the 7/11 blasts. I do not know what the Lashkar is. I remember that I had stated that I had met one person by the name of Tariq, and not Faisal. I was brought by the ATS to Mumbai in connection with the statements that I made on television,' Hashmi said.

Though Hashmi retracted almost everything he had said in the past, he confidently accepted being a part of the Al-Badr. He said he had been in Chella Bandi, a training ground of the Hizb-ul-Mujahideen. But he did not accept the ATS's assertion that he met Faisal there.

'I am not afraid of Lashkar-e-Taiba as I have no connection with it. I do not know whether the objectives of Lashkar-e-Taiba and Al-Badr are the same. Al-Badr is not against India. Its objective is to give freedom to Kashmir. I do not know any other organizations having the same objective. The reason for the anti-India sentiment in Pakistan may be because of border dispute and the wars,' he reasoned.

Hashmi claimed that he had no information or knowledge about the train blasts till the Mumbai ATS arrested him. He also accused the ATS of pressuring him into giving a statement. But he said he could not recall the names of the officers who had pressurized him to do so. Hashmi said he had seen the accused being tortured during his time in Bhoiwada. He narrated how Faisal's youngest brother, Muzzammil, was beaten with a hunter inside the cell, while another detainee lay naked with severe injuries on his back.

Hashmi said that he feared being implicated in a false case and, therefore, out of fear he signed every document the police gave him at that time. He added that the ATS had promised to send him back home if he did as they said. Following his deposition, Hashmi was sent back to the Srinagar jail to serve the rest of his sentence for his involvement in terror activities in Kashmir.

10

Terror Revisits

'Nanha munna rahi hoon, desh ka sipahi hoon . . .'. Six-year-old Mohammad Aasir, sporting a bloodied bandage around his head, hummed, standing outside Noor Hospital in Malegaon. The biggest hospital in this communally sensitive town in Nashik district was overcrowded with injured people and dead bodies, for a bomb had exploded in the city's busy streets, killing thirty-eight people. Among the dead were Aasir's two older brothers and an uncle.

At that early age, Aasir had witnessed death and terror first-hand.

It was 8 September 2006, just two months after the deadly terror attacks on Mumbai's Western Railway trains. And terror had struck again, this time 290 kilometres away from Mumbai, in this little power-loom town. It was Shab-e-Baraat, a special day in the Muslim calendar, when the devout pay respects to the dead. It was also a Friday and the Hamidiya mosque inside Bada Kabristan was full of people who had gathered for the afternoon prayers.

At 1.50 p.m., three bombs went off within minutes of each other, just as the crowd was leaving after offering prayers.

A stampede-like situation broke out after the blasts as panic-stricken devotees, including women and children, ran outside in the ensuing confusion. The first bomb was placed at the entrance of the Bada Kabristan compound, the second on a bicycle in the parking lot and the third one was hung on the wall of the power-supply room in front of the *vaju khana* (the place where men cleanse themselves before offering namaz). The fourth blast was at Mushawarat Chowk nearby, in the heart of Malegaon. The bomb was placed on a bicycle near an electric pole.

The injured were rushed to hospitals using every available mode of transport, some even wheeled on pushcarts lying nearby. Among the casualties were several beggars who had lined up outside the cemetery to collect alms, knowing that people are usually generous after Friday prayers.

Treatment of the injured had only started in the hospital when a mob tore through the town, pelting stones and shouting slogans to protest what had happened. This rampage was seen as a deliberate attempt to disrupt the communal harmony of the town. Malegaon, home to a large Muslim population, had apparently been targeted to incite communal disharmony. A curfew was announced, and paramilitary forces and the police fanned into sensitive areas, trying to maintain peace. No terrorist organization claimed responsibility for the blasts.

Back in Mumbai, where the probe into the 7/11 train blasts was still midway, the Malegaon explosions created a flutter. ATS chief K.P. Raghuvanshi and his team left for Malegaon immediately. On arrival, he decided to keep a small investigating team stationed in town to keep vigil. He also announced that the investigating team would study past communal clashes and terror-related activities in the area.

Because of their recent setbacks in piecing together the conspiracy behind the Mumbai bomb blasts, the ATS was trying to improve its intelligence-gathering machinery. The squad had also undergone a major revamp at the senior level, with new IPS officers being posted to the ATS. ACP Kisan Shengal who was coordinating directly with the investigators on the field in Mumbai was deployed to Malegaon. He went on to supervise the investigations there.

Curfew, imposed on 8 September, was lifted the next morning as devotees, undeterred by the terror blitz, bowed their heads in prayer again.

It was too early for investigators to deal with another blast. All they knew for certain was that there had been four bombs, not three as reported earlier. They admitted that they could not find any leads at the blast sites. Senior officials pointed out the possibility of RDX being used as the primary ingredient in the bombs, a marked similarity with the 7/11 train blasts. Preliminary investigations further indicated that these low-intensity bombs contained iron shrapnel and ball bearings, usually the ingredients in an Improvised Explosive Device (IED) designed to cause maximum casualties. The explosives were fitted with timers.

The first job at hand was to trace the owners of the bicycles used in the blasts. A special team of ten members, comprising ATS officers, a case detection squad of the Malegaon police and other officers on deputation was formed. Samples from the blast sites had already been collected and sent to the Forensic Sciences Laboratory in Kalina. Residents blamed the police for poor bandobast that Friday. The police, in turn, blamed the locals, saying the management of the cemetery did not want the force present on Shab-e-Baraat. This was only the beginning of the blame game.

Two days after the blasts, investigators came up with the sketches of two suspects seen parking bicycles at the spots of the crime. Amidst a public outcry over the incident, the police declared that a breakthrough had been made—they said the cycles had been purchased from two shops in the city.

This announcement was pivotal, for the bicycles had been bought just three hours before the blasts on Friday and the sketches of the two men who purchased them were being released.

The revelations were timely. Senior officers were already struggling to pacify angry citizens, assuring them that the accused would be arrested soon. This announcement was projected as a headway in the case.

By Sunday, a fragile peace prevailed in the area, though most shops remained closed and the streets were deserted. Law enforcers spent long hours away from home, either manning their offices or keeping a tense vigil on the streets.

Investigating agencies were soon faced with a new angle in the probe: the role of Hindu extremist groups behind the attacks. Just two days after the blasts, the Maharashtra police, so focused on Islamic terrorist organizations, were reluctant to change the direction of their suspicions. Much like their narrow approach, their dossiers were limited to the idea of Muslim fundamentalists.

Nevertheless, a few officers begged to differ. Abraham Mathai, head of the State Minority Commission, wrote a letter to the state director general of police, pointing out possible similarities between the explosives used in the Malegaon case and those used in the Nanded and Jalna attacks in 2002 and 2003 respectively. The suggestion was that the timing of the attack indicated that it could be the handiwork of a group seeking to target the Muslim community. Unfortunately, investigations into the conspiracies behind the attacks at Nanded, Jalna and Parbhani in 2002 and 2003 had yet to yield any concrete results. The Bajrang Dal's name had been bandied about in connection with some attacks, but investigators were unable to pinpoint any right-wing masterminds behind the explosions.

The ATS had initially ruled out the possibility of a Hindu outfit behind the blasts, for two main reasons. One, they claimed RDX was available 'only' to Muslim terrorists. Two, until then, Bajrang Dal activists had allegedly only used crude bombs.

Meanwhile, the Urdu press, reflecting popular sentiment in Malegaon, criticized the investigating agencies for their inability to prevent Friday's blasts. Almost every Urdu newspaper in the city highlighted the plight of the community. The government's reactions to the blast came under sharp criticism too, with a dramatic front-page editorial of *Urdu Times* reading, '*Ab Musalmano ka Allah hi hafiz*' (Now god is the only protector of Muslims). Mumbai's leading Urdu daily, *Inquilab*, alleged that authorities and the national media wasted no time in pointing fingers at certain Muslim organizations, while ignoring the similarities between the Malegaon attack and the blasts in Parbhani and Jalna. All the blasts had taken place outside mosques between 1.45 p.m. and 2 p.m. on Friday, a day that witnesses maximum attendance.

~

Two days after the blasts, the local police received a preliminary report from the forensic department revealing that a timer device with a printed circuit board had been installed in the four bombs. An Orpat alarm clock was used as the timer.

Once the forensic reports were in, two more teams were sent to Malegaon for further investigations. The police also met the trustees of the city's mosques and temples, advising them to appoint their own watchmen who could be trained by the police.

Then, a week after the blasts, the investigators were sent into a tizzy when reports of an unexploded bomb in a shopping complex in Malegaon surfaced. They acted swiftly, with the bomb squad rushing to the spot along with their sniffer dogs to locate the bomb, which was placed on a projecting window near a staircase. The squad carefully moved the package from the complex to a closed municipal school nearby. Around 2.30 p.m., a team of National Security Guard (NSG) experts was called in from Nashik. Six hours later, it was discovered that the 'bomb' was nothing but mud mixed with gunpowder, packed in a sweet box. The hoax was a clear indication of the intent to provoke trouble in a city with a history of communal discord.

It would be another two weeks before the police found concrete evidence. With over 400 suspects questioned and the statements of all the witnesses recorded, the police now claimed to have specific information about the perpetrators. Six teams of policemen were sent out of town, in pursuit of leads and suspects.

In Mumbai, the investigators in the train blasts case suddenly announced that the Malegaon blasts probe had provided them with vital leads. In fact, it was assumed that the same set of terrorists had carried out the blasts in Mumbai as well as in Malegaon. The director general of police, Parvinder Singh Pasricha, was reported saying that the explosives used in both blasts were similar and that the two attacks were linked. The police also found that the explosives used in the Malegaon blasts were a cocktail of RDX, ammonium nitrate and fuel oil, the same combination used in the Mumbai train blasts.

The investigators were more convinced now that three important cases, all within two months of each other, were interlinked—the Aurangabad arms haul, the 7/11 serial train blasts and the Malegaon blasts. The LeT was accused of being behind all the three cases. Faisal, one of the prime accused in 7/11 case, was charged with helping an accused flee the country in the Aurangabad arms haul case. A more concrete link between the Aurangabad arms haul and the 7/11 case could never be established, however, for there was never enough proof.

Officials also claimed that Faisal had sent one Fayyaz Kagzi for training to Pakistan in the past, who, along with Rahil Shaikh, was wanted in the Aurangabad arms haul and the Mumbai train blasts. They added that Faisal was in direct touch with the Pakistani jihadi boss, Azam Cheema, based in Bahawalpur.

～

Claiming that the Malegaon blasts were the handiwork of SIMI activists, on 30 October the state police made the first arrest in the case—that of Noor-ul-Huda Shamsuddoha, a labourer in a battery unit in Malegaon. Shabbir Masiullah, the owner of the unit where Shamsuddoha worked, was also arrested later. Masiullah was not an unfamiliar face for the police. He had already been arrested by the Mumbai Crime Branch for his SIMI links in August 2006—just a month before the Malegaon blasts. At the time of his arrest, Shamsuddoha was already in custody and was accused of planting the fake bomb at the shopping complex in Malegaon. He had been arrested on

9 October under the UAPA. When the police later collected mud samples from Masiullah's factory, they claimed to have found the same traces of the explosives used in the dummy bomb.

The hunt now moved on to people who had actually planted the bombs at the four locations. Shamsuddoha was small fry; the main perpetrators were still at large. The police revealed that the bomb conspiracy for the blasts had been hatched eight months ago at Shamsuddoha's wedding, while RDX was smuggled into Malegaon by a separate module.

Masiullah was named the brain behind the blasts, while Shamsuddoha was considered a mere pawn. The bombs used in the blasts were made in Masiullah's factory in the last week of July. He told the police that he knew the other planters too, but did not know their real names or identities. It was clear that more than half a dozen people were involved in this case.

After the 7/11 bombings, Shamsuddoha was picked up from Malegaon by the Mumbai Crime Branch and detained for questioning at unit 7 between 4 August and 14 August. He was released later when the police failed to find any evidence against him.

Weeks after Masiullah and Shamsuddoha were arrested, the ATS picked up two more accused from the 7/11 case—Govandi resident Mohammed Ali Alam Shaikh and SIMI executive Asif Bashir Khan, alias Junaid. This brought on record the 'links' between the 7/11 and Malegaon cases—that the leftover RDX from Mumbai serial train bombings was used in the Malegaon blasts and was arranged by Mohammed Ali and Asif. Moreover, most of the accused arrested in the two blast cases were current or former members of SIMI.

It was revealed that the bombs planted on the Mumbai suburban trains had been assembled at Mohammed Ali's

Govandi house. Both Mohammed Ali and Asif had also transported the explosives to Malegaon, which were later used in the four bombs that went off on 8 September. The Malegaon conspiracy had been hatched on 8 May when all of the conspirators had met at Shamsuddoha's wedding. The RDX was transported from Mumbai to Malegaon in the third week of July, right after the train blasts. One more accused, Dr Salman Farsi, was arrested for the Malegaon blasts.

At least 15 kilograms of RDX had been transported to Malegaon, safely hidden in Masiullah's godown. Only 1.5 to 2 kilograms of RDX was used to make the four bombs— the remaining quantity was yet to be traced. The police also revealed that a Pakistani national had come to Malegaon to make the bombs.

Investigators finally filed a charge sheet in the Malegaon blasts case in December that year after arresting nine men, most of them from Malegaon.

There were similarities galore between the 7/11 serial train blasts case and the Malegaon case, in terms of a similar set of accused being arrested, use of explosives and the Pakistan angle. However, two and a half years later, these cases would take two completely different directions, with the Malegaon case going on to become the most unique in the history of criminal cases in this country.

11

Preparation and Execution

30 September 2006

It was the day not just Mumbai but the entire nation was waiting for with bated breath. Over eleven weeks after the 7/11 serial train blasts, the state police had called the biggest press conference in their history to announce that they had solved the case.

The presser was at the Azad Maidan Police Club, a venue usually reserved for the city police's annual press conference and meetings conducted by high-ranking police officials with heads of local police stations. A slew of senior officials—State Director General of Police Parvinder Singh Pasricha, Mumbai Police Commissioner A.N. Roy, ATS chief Krish Pal Raghuvanshi and several additional commissioners of police sat on the stage.

The size of the venue enabled a large media presence, and journalists from across the country and world crowded the room. Over twenty television cameras formed an arc in front of the stage, most connected to outside broadcast (OB) vans to telecast the conference live. Around fifty pairs of eyes were fixed on the stage, waiting for the announcement to be made.

'It has been a beautiful piece of highly professional investigation conducted by our team,' Roy said, looking proud of the police's accomplishment. The blasts were the work of Pakistan's Inter-Services Intelligence, which had worked with the Lashkar-e-Taiba, the police explained at the conference. The LeT had executed the plan with help from the banned Students Islamic Movement of India. Close to two months before the blasts, twelve perpetrators from Pakistan had sneaked into India through the borders of Bangladesh, Nepal and Gujarat. One of them carried 15–20 kilograms of the deadly explosive RDX. The bombs were placed in pressure cookers covered by newspapers and umbrellas, and triggered by a timer device. The attackers moved in pairs—one Indian and one Pakistani. Seven pairs planted seven bombs in seven trains. After the blasts, ten of the twelve Pakistanis had probably gone back through the porous borders, while two others were killed—one in the train blast and the other in a police encounter. Fifteen men had been arrested until the press conference.

The police had first arrested Kamal Ansari through an analysis of phone calls made from Mumbai. The arrests of Faisal Atta-ur Rahman Shaikh, Dr Tanveer Ansari, Ehtesham Siddiqui, Abdul Wahideen Mohammad Shaikh, Naved Hussain Khan, Tafheem Akmal Hashmi, Khalid Aziz Shaikh, Mumtaz Ahmed Chaudhary, Muzzammil Shaikh, Zameer Shaikh, Suhail Shaikh, Mohammed Majid Shafi, Mohammed Ali Shaikh and Sajid Ansari followed. The police admitted that the case against Pakistani soldier Tafheem Akmal Hashmi, Kamal's relative Mumtaz Chaudhary and friend Khalid Shaikh was weak. Azam Cheema, Rizwan Dawrey and

Rahil Shaikh were named the main perpetrators, but were still at large. Subsequently, the police made two more arrests. Asif Bashir Khan was arrested three days later, on 3 October.

Strangely, there were several differences between the revelations made by the police during the press conference and the details mentioned in the charge sheet filed exactly two months after the press conference, on 30 November.

The 10,667-pages charge sheet was a voluminous reminder of the ghastly crime that had killed 187 people until then; it contained minute details of the crime with statements of 2200 witnesses. The ATS sleuths often gazed at the pile of papers neatly stashed on their desks and wondered about the enormity of the task at hand. Every word typed on the charge sheet painted a picture of what had happened in the months leading up to the violence and on the day of the blasts. Their investigation had, according to them, laid bare the entire conspiracy, and the sordid saga of violence and vengeance. The charge sheet explained that though the terror attack on Mumbai was in the works for years, since the 2002 Gujarat riots, the foundation for an assault on Mumbai's trains was laid in February, beginning with a spine-chilling message from Azam Cheema.

~

'Main apne dus–barah admi aur RDX, dono bhej raha hoon, taiyyar rehna (I am sending ten–twelve men and RDX. Be prepared),' the message read. It reached Faisal at the end of February 2006. The message meant that making arrangements for the stay of the men from Pakistan and coordinating with them was Faisal's responsibility. It also meant that Cheema was not relying only on Indians to carry out the attack.

The LeT had spent a lot of money on Faisal and, until now, he had received more than Rs 10 lakh from Cheema. Of this, he had managed to deposit Rs 2 lakh in his father's account. After the message from Cheema, Faisal recalled the Rs 1.80 lakh he had received the first time he returned from Pakistan in 2002. What a long way he had come since then, he thought. This money had helped Faisal rent the flat in Bandra, away from his parents in Mira Road and away from the prying eyes of the police. Dawrey and Rahil, both of whom were based in Saudi Arabia now, facilitated all the hawala money transactions from Pakistan. Once it reached India, Faisal would mostly keep the money with his cousin sister, Khalida, who lived in Temkar Mohalla, opposite Pakmodia Street, where the notorious don Dawood Ibrahim resided before he fled the country. For his work in the train bomb blasts, Faisal was to receive 11,200 riyals, roughly Rs 1,45,000.

By now, Faisal had already convinced Asif, Ehtesham, Tanveer, Suhail, Zameer and Muzzammil to take part in the terror conspiracy. He had met Asif and Ehtesham in the many countrywide programmes organized by SIMI, which continued even after the ban on the organization. Asif and Ehtesham were keen on setting up a base to train SIMI men in India itself, instead of being tools in the hands of the Pakistanis. Ehtesham refused to go to Pakistan for training even when Faisal offered to fund him. Instead, Ehtesham convinced Tanveer to go. Until the plan to set up training camps in India materialized, Ehtesham and Asif had decided to help Faisal.

The money that Faisal got from the LeT helped him lure more accomplices in the attack. One of these was Mohammed Ali Alam Shaikh—a short, calm man with a long beard, its tips dyed with henna. An ex-SIMI member, and extremely short of cash at that time, he had approached Riyaz Bhatkal, also an ex-SIMI activist, who is well known in the Indian Islamic terror network, for money to start a business. Riyaz sent Mohammed Ali to Pakistan for training and paid him through a colleague, Asif Razak. Soon after, Razak died in a police encounter and payments to Mohammed Ali stopped. Mohammed Ali, in dire straits, started to sell *tilasmi moti* (magical pearls) in the M.H. Saboo Siddique Hospital to earn a living. At this time, Tanveer practised at the same hospital and Faisal frequently visited him. Mohammed Ali met Faisal through Tanveer. After a few meetings, Faisal decided that Mohammed Ali, who seemed dedicated and in need of money, could be used for odd jobs.

But Faisal did not spend all the money he received from the LeT on the attack. He also spent a large part of it on himself—the flat he lived in, the women he met and his friends. Faisal could often be found on the Carter Road Promenade, at the newest eatery in the city or spending time at bars with his closest friends, Naved and Mohammad Alam Qureshi. Faisal was a teetotaller, but enjoyed soft drinks and the company of women. He also spent some money on Manisha, whom he had fallen in love with, after he saw her dancing at Sai Dance Plaza.

Naved, Faisal's friend, had recently moved to Mumbai for a new job and lived in Mira Road with his brother, a copy editor at a national English daily. Naved, a stylish young man who sported a goatee, was a cleanliness freak. He had lived in Hyderabad since 2004 and had worked in several multinationals. During one of his visits to the city, Faisal invited Naved to meet Ehtesham, Asif and Tanveer. Faisal's friend Qureshi was not a part of the terrorist attack, but attended most meetings at Faisal's house, even though Asif resented Qureshi's presence. These meetings were secret and the discussion mostly religious. Soon, Naved was convinced to help Faisal in the execution of the blasts.

~

Mumbai, a bustling city of 15 million people, is often considered a country within a country. It is called the 'Dream City of India' and attracts lakhs of people each year, all of them hoping to make it big. Unlike Delhi and Chandigarh, both planned cities that are geographically circular, Mumbai has grown linearly. As such, lakhs of people from the distant suburbs travel towards central and south Mumbai for work and leisure. It is the only city in India with this kind of a linear structure.

A 319-kilometre suburban rail system runs down the length of Mumbai and is the most direct, or rather the most convenient, mass transit system connecting the suburbs to the commercial centre of Mumbai. The rail transport system is divided into two sections—Western and Central, which is made up of the Central and Harbour railway lines. In addition to the suburban rail system, some state trains and some trains from India's national railway network also use the same railway tracks. The Mumbai rail network is one of the busiest systems in the world, with over 2500 daily train services—a train leaves every three minutes. Trains run all day, except for three hours between 1 a.m. and 4 a.m.

But this train system is choked beyond its capacity, with over 70 lakh daily travellers. Trains provide a faster travel option to the millions hurrying to work or home, especially since small distances could take several hours to cover by road due to traffic snarls and the pothole-ridden roads. The crowd during peak hours in the morning and evening would shock even the Chinese, who have the world's longest high-speed rail network. With an 8358-kilometre-long high-speed rail network, with speeds as high as 350 kilometres per hour, places such as Beijing and Shanghai have 200 train services a day, compared to CST, which sees 600 train services a day. Moreover, most of the trains are of inferior quality when compared to the technologically advanced Chinese ones.

～

This rail network provided the LeT, Faisal and his coterie, an excellent opportunity to adversely impact the lives of Mumbai's citizens and businesses, primarily the Gujarati community. One night in May, Faisal smirked as he thought of the targets they had shortlisted. Crowded, cluttered and lacking security. Beggars, drug addicts, criminals, traders, everyone could use the local trains of Mumbai without being questioned. These were the perfect terror targets.

But things weren't going well for Faisal. Cheema's men would land up at his doorstep soon and Faisal had begun to fret. He didn't know the dates they would arrive in the city and he didn't have a place for them to stay or a plan to help them make and plant the bombs. He still needed to scope out the targets. Faisal didn't want to tick off the man sitting in Bahawalpur once again. It was time to act or they would lose this opportunity.

First, Faisal asked Tanveer, Ehtesham, Muzzammil, Suhail and Zameer to study their targets.

The western rail corridor that they planned to bomb stretched from Churchgate in the south to Virar on the fringes of the city, and covered a distance of 60 kilometres. The line had twenty-eight stations on it. As many as 30 lakh people commuted southwards in the morning and returned home in the evening, using the same corridor. People living in the western suburbs were, on average, richer than those living on the Central and Harbour railway lines. So the Western Line saw more elite passengers.

Early in May, Faisal, Tanveer, Ehtesham, Suhail, Muzzammil and Zameer had gone to Churchgate station, bought tickets from the counter and boarded the Virar-bound local trains. Faisal and Zameer got into one train and took position at either door of one compartment. Ehtesham, Suhail, Muzzammil and Zameer took window seats in different trains. They smiled at the posters of godmen promising solutions to various problems—financial, marital and emotional—that decorated the compartments. The usual crowd in the trains had thinned by the afternoon. The six could sit and think, and scan every corner of the compartment. By the time they returned to Churchgate, the rush was palpable. People squeezed themselves in to the general compartment until there was barely any space to breathe. The first-class compartment, reserved for people who paid a higher fare, caught their attention. Most commuters looked like they came from richer families and no one would agree to share a three-person seat with a fourth person, a practice usually followed in the second-class general compartments. But during the rush hours of the morning and evening, there was little difference between a first-class and general compartment. The first-class compartments would make a better target than the general coaches, the six decided.

Their next task was figuring out who would make the bombs. Faisal asked Tanveer if he knew how to make bombs with RDX, only to be told that he only knew how to make liquid bombs, which contain everyday liquid chemicals. It had been so long since their training in Pakistan that most of them did not remember the details of how to make a bomb. But Faisal was not relying completely on these six men. The terrorists from Pakistan would make the bombs and Faisal only needed someone to assist them. Someone suggested the name of Sajid, a young man recently elected the president of the Mira Road unit of SIMI and owner of a mobile-repair shop in Jogeshwari. He could be helpful in connecting the circuits for the bombs.

The next meeting was the most crucial one. Faisal, along with Asif, had decided to assign tasks to each of them. They had decided by now that they would bomb seven first-class compartments of the Mumbai locals during rush hour. Zameer, Tanveer, Muzzammil and Suhail were to remain on standby, while the bombs would be planted by Faisal, Ehtesham, Asif, Naved and Kamal. The next task on hand was taking care of the Pakistanis. 'Who will take the responsibility of their hospitality?' asked Faisal. This was not the first time Faisal had raised this issue. The idea of housing so many Pakistanis frightened him. Tanveer told Faisal that he should go ahead and house them in the room he had suggested in February. But the security deposit for that flat was too high. Faisal asked Mohammed Ali if he could accommodate a few Pakistanis at his place. 'I stay in a very tiny house in Govandi with my family. How can I make anyone stay with me there?' Mohammed Ali demurred. Faisal acquiesced, but decided that Govandi was an ideal place for making the bombs. Ehtesham volunteered to scrutinize the premises.

It wasn't very often that such logistical details occupied Faisal's mind, but hosting the Pakistanis was an issue that needed to be addressed urgently. In addition, it would be difficult to host so many of them at his house. This was when Asif stepped in. He hadn't been around a lot especially because he was wanted by the police in a couple of cases and had to be careful at all times. But things were moving fast now. Eventually, during the whole process of planning the blasts and taking care of the Pakistanis, Asif had been a rock for Faisal to lean on and he was extremely thankful for his presence.

Finally, the group decided that most of the Pakistanis would stay with Faisal, and Asif would make arrangements for the rest of them.

~

Abdul Razzak from Hyderabad, whom Faisal had met during his first training in Pakistan, had arrived in the city in May 2006 through the Kutch border, along with Salim, Abu Umed and Sohail. Razzak had followed Faisal's trajectory from his first time in Pakistan and was here to accompany him on his first attack on the kafirs. Sohail Shaikh was from Pune, but had lived in Pakistan since the early 2000s. He had trained with Faisal for four months in 2003.

The second group of terrorists from Pakistan reached the next day, and entered India with the help of Abdul Rehman and Kamal. Abdul Rehman was an LeT operative tasked with the job of ferrying recruits to Pakistan from Iran for training.

Kamal had reluctantly agreed to help the LeT with the bomb blasts. Kamal was not a SIMI man. His connection with Faisal's group was through the LeT, who exploited him for their own purposes, preying on his need for money. Years ago, Kamal had been forced by Hafiz Zuber, an LeT operative in Nepal, to cross the border into Pakistan and collect donations for madrasas. But once Kamal crossed the border, he was sent to training camps instead and was told about the atrocities committed against Muslim women in India. He trained in the deserts of Bahawalpur with AK-47s, rifles and bombs. He was sent back, completely brainwashed, and told that he could make a lot of money if he convinced young boys to undergo training and wage jihad under the guise of collecting donations. On his way back to his village, Kamal was arrested in Delhi for possessing a rifle and no one bailed him out.

Disillusioned, Kamal was not keen to work for the LeT. This time, when Hafiz Zuber invited Kamal for a meeting, he tempted him with money. Kamal agreed and met Abdul Rehman in Nepal, and returned to Madhubani, a village in Bihar, with Rs 10,000, half a kilogram of RDX and two Pakistanis—Aslam and Hafizullah. He took the material and the men to Mumbai on a train. The other passengers on the train viewed the trio with curiosity. All three men were 6-feet tall and the two Pakistanis looked very foreign. Kamal dropped them off at a shop in Jogeshwari owned by one Sajid chacha. The Pakistanis were to stay at Sajid's house in Saba Parveen Apartment in Mira Road. Kamal returned to Bihar, but was instructed to be in Mumbai during the attacks.

A third man, Mohammed Majid Shafi, a shoe shop owner from Kolkata, was responsible for ferrying six Pakistanis into and out of India through the Bangladesh border. Majid, slightly stout and fair, was a reserved man. He was under the influence of Mohammad Asif, his wealthy cousin who was an LeT loyalist. Majid had once helped a few men cross into India from Bangladesh. 'What are you doing with your life? There is a higher calling that you are required for,' Mohammed Asif had told him, goading him to do something in the name of god. This time Mohammad Asif convinced Majid to help the LeT. 'Azam Cheema is working for god's will and so is Abdul Razzak. You must help them in their mission to destroy Mumbai,' Asif had told Majid.

During the third week of May, Majid told his childhood friend and business partner, Shakil Mehboob, to receive some men at Bangaon, a town on the border of India and Bangladesh. Mehboob owed Majid some money, so he agreed to help him. At the Bangaon market area, six men in their twenties—Abu Bakr, Sabir, Kasam Ali, Ammu Jaan, Abu Hasan and Ehsanullah—were waiting for Majid. The hefty-looking men were all carrying their own bags. Ehsanullah's bag was unusually large. When he noticed Majid looking at him, he grinned and said, 'The bag contains enough RDX to bomb the entire city.' The men took a train to Kolkata and then took another one to Mumbai from there.

Majid was nervous around these men and the RDX. He was anxious to meet Asif in Mumbai and hand these men over to him. Two days later, the group reached Mumbai, where they met Asif at Amrapali Apartments, his residence in Thane. Majid returned to Kolkata.

~

All of Faisal's 'guests' had now arrived in Mumbai. He had forgotten the last time he had visited a bar. One evening, he called up Qureshi and Naved, and asked them to accompany him to a bar for the last time. There was a hint of finality in his voice. Faisal sneaked out of the house, dressed in his best, but still wearing his everyday cap. The trio travelled in a second-hand white Maruti 800, purchased recently by his youngest brother, Muzzammil. Music blared from the radio in the car, as Naved drove at breakneck speed. After a night of revelry, the three of them returned to Faisal's home early in the morning. There wasn't enough space for everyone in the house and Faisal believed that the crowd might make the neighbours suspicious.

He asked Naved the first of many favours, to shift the Pakistanis elsewhere. Naved obliged; they were shifted to a safe hideout in Millat Nagar in Andheri, another Mumbai suburb.

The evening before the group started making the bombs, Faisal and Naved drove down to Carter Road. On the promenade, Tanveer, Ehtesham and Zameer waited for them. It was a regular evening, with five friends enjoying the cool breeze and the calming smell of the sea. They spoke about life, about their families and about their hopes and dreams.

~

On 8 July, in a room measuring 15x10 feet in a narrow Govandi by-lane, Mohammed Ali had made arrangements for making the bombs. He had moved his family to a relative's house in Rafiq Nagar on Faisal's instructions. Naved and Faisal dropped Sajid off at the Govandi house and returned to Faisal's apartment. For the next three days, the group remained hard at work. Tanveer stood guard outside the shanty, while Ehtesham and Asif supervised the making of the bombs. Mohammed Ali stood by, ready to assist Sajid and a few of the Pakistanis, including Sohail, who were making the bombs. Newspapers, batteries, wires, printed circuit boards, a soldering gun, resistors, capacitors and insulation tape, everything was laid out on the floor. A few days ago, Asif had delivered eight black-coloured Rexine bags for the bombs along with ammonium nitrate, detonators, cords and watches to Mohammed Ali's house. Sohail, the bomb expert, mixed ammonium nitrate, RDX and diesel to prepare the explosives; he then fixed the detonators and a timer device. Sajid joined the circuit and wires. Everything was going just fine until the arrival of Aman Khan.

Khan, who hailed from the Mumbai suburb of Vikhroli and was a former SIMI activist, wanted to purchase raw material to make plaster of Paris, a business he had been dealing in for years. On their way to the shop, he and his friend Ajmeri Shaikh passed by Mohammed Ali's house. Since they knew Mohammed Ali, they stopped their bike and went to meet him. But Mohammed Ali, standing at the doorstep, did not seem pleased to see them. He whispered urgently to Tanveer, who was manning the entry of the shanty, and returned inside the house. Mystified, Khan peeked inside. Mohammed Ali panicked when he saw him and asked him to leave immediately. He insisted he was busy with some important work and would meet Khan later. Insulted, Khan and Shaikh left the house.

~

The bombs were ready on 10 July. The group cleaned the house thoroughly, put the bombs in Rexine bags and carried all seven bags to Faisal's house—four bags in the boot of the white Maruti car, and the remaining bags in a black-and-yellow taxi, a staple on Mumbai's roads.

On 11 July, Ehtesham, Naved, Asif and Kamal, with their Pakistani counterparts—Hafizullah, Aslam, Salim, Ammu Jaan, Abu Umed, Sabir and Abu Bakr—gathered at Faisal's house on Perry Cross Road at 3 p.m. 'Do not carry your phones,' the handlers from the LeT had instructed them. They were also supposed to ignore each other even if they met at the station. At 3.30 p.m., Faisal indicated that Ehtesham should leave the building.

'Khuda hafiz,' Ehtesham said, as his Pakistani counterpart Ammu Jaan lifted the bomb-laden bag. They took a taxi to

Churchgate station and got off near the subway that led to the platforms. As they emerged from the subway, they felt lost, unsure about what to do. Ehtesham, almost out of reflex, asked the man on his right, 'This is the Virar 5.19, right?' As the Virar-bound train pulled into the platform, they knew it had all begun. The duo stepped into the train with the bag full of explosives.

Faisal and Abu Bakr were the last ones to leave the house. They occupied the back seat of the taxi and kept their Rexine bag on the passenger seat in the front. Faisal feared the bomb would malfunction and that they would become the first casualties of the blasts. 'Do you want me to put it in the boot?' asked the taxi driver. 'No,' said Faisal curtly. The taxi ride was silent—no one uttered another word after that. When the taxi was crossing Prabhadevi, Faisal looked at the iconic Siddhivinayak temple and thought of how, just a few months ago, they were grappling with the idea of finding targets to attack. At Churchgate, the duo handed over Rs 150 to the driver and did not take the change back.

Like Ehtesham, Faisal took the subway and entered the first-class compartment of the Borivali slow train, scheduled to depart in a few minutes. Faisal did not want to hold on to the bag in his hands, but there was no space in the crowded luggage racks above the seats. He slid the bag under his seat. Faisal noticed he was the only person to put the bag beneath the seat. Everyone else had kept their bags on the rack above. His mind raced. What if someone questioned him if he got off without taking his bag? What if the bomb exploded before he could get off the train?

When Naved left to plant the bomb, he handed over his mobile phone to Sajid outside Lucky Restaurant in Bandra. After stopping at Faisal's house to pick up the explosive-laden bag, he and his Pakistani partner, Abu Umed, headed to Churchgate station. Naved reached early and first headed to the ticket counter to buy two first-class tickets. He navigated the evening rush at the station and entered the train standing on platform no. 2. He put the bag in the luggage rack above and pushed it as far from him as possible. Both of them got off the train at Dadar railway station.

Asif's Virar fast train had already left the platform at Churchgate station. An umbrella in one hand, he tried to pretend like he was a regular commuter. His Pakistani counterpart, Sabir, seemed nervous. They placed the bomb-laden Rexine bag on the rack above the seat in a compartment so packed, there was no space to breathe. Asif's thoughts went to the Rs 500 note he had handed over to the taxi driver because he couldn't find change in his pocket for the Rs 180 fare. How could I have not been prepared for this? What if the driver suspects something? he thought nervously. They had reached their compartment only in the nick of time. He wondered how the others were faring.

By now, the crowd had increased further—people rushed into the compartments, trying to get home to their loved ones, watch their favourite television show or reach in time to finish a household chore.

The 5.57 p.m. Virar fast, which Kamal, Salim, Hafizullah and Aslam had boarded, was the last to leave the station. After placing the bomb, only three of them made their way out of the train. The incoming crowd at Dadar station had started pushing their way inside so quickly that Salim could not make his way out. When Kamal realized what had happened, he sat down on the platform and clutched his head. One of them had been left to die in the train. It was just minutes before the blast.

All of the bombers were in a hurry to head back home. Kamal, who had come to Mumbai for the attacks, dropped the three Pakistanis at Sajid's Mira Road house and took the night train to Patna from Kalyan. He reached his village in Bihar by 13 July.

Majid, from Kolkata, was called in to ferry Abu Bakr, Sabir, Kasam Ali, Ammu Jaan, Abu Hasan and Ehsanullah back to the border. He had reached Mumbai a day before the blasts. Asif asked him to spend the night at the house of Abdul Wahideen Mohammad Shaikh, another SIMI member who had been arrested during the 2001 SIMI crackdown. Majid obliged. Abdul Wahid was Sajid's brother-in-law and one of the smartest in the group. Abdul Wahid's house had been used for several meetings in the past. Wahid's relative would diligently hand over their house keys to Ehtesham while they were away. After the blasts, Majid and the six Pakistanis fled to Gujarat in the darkness of the night. Later, they took a train to Kolkata and crossed the border to Bangladesh.

Abu Umed, who had planted the bomb along with Naved, was dropped off near Faisal's house. But he never went to Faisal's house. Instead, he left for Antop Hill, where he was eventually killed in the police encounter. The residents of Mumbai took buses out of the city and melted into the crowd. Faisal was entrusted with 15,000 riyals that was to be distributed among the Indians. But before the money could reach them, Faisal was caught and the cash was seized.

The next time they met each other was in prison.

12

A Bomb for a Bomb

A C-130 from the Pakistan Air Force landed in Delhi on 23 February 2007. Sixty-two people, all Pakistani citizens, had to be airlifted back to safety. These were the people injured, mourning the loss of loved ones, each one of them regretting their visit to India. Just days earlier, the Samjhauta Express, the only train to run between India and Pakistan, had been bombed by terrorists—the two bogies, and a promising symbol of compromise between the two countries, destroyed in one fell swoop.

The powerful explosion on 18 February ripped apart the two carriages, both mostly carrying Pakistanis back to their homeland. The explosion had left sixty-eight dead and scores wounded, and threatened to end the nascent and fragile peace process.

The explosion was followed by a massive fire that engulfed coaches 10 and 11. The deaths were on account of burns and suffocation. Among the injured, twenty were critical and were rushed to the civil hospital for treatment. Several passengers, including women, children and senior citizens, jumped out of the burning train, even as it continued to move forward. Fire engines were rushed to the spot, but it took two hours before they could bring the fire under control.

The timing of the attack was strategic. The following day, on 19 February 2007, India and Pakistan were scheduled to resume peace talks. The intention of the attackers was obvious to all.

Having left Old Delhi railway station, the train was on its way to Attari, the last station on the Indian side of the border 25 kilometres ahead of Amritsar, from where the last few passengers boarded the train to Lahore. From Attari, Lahore is just 30 kilometres away. Investigations would reveal later that IEDs fitted with timers were used in the blasts and that the bombs were placed in suitcases hidden in the compartments. A suitcase would be recovered the following day from another coach with two more IEDs that had to be defused. The plan was diabolical—more coaches had been targeted. Finally, eight remaining coaches were allowed to continue the journey the next day, but the convivial spirit in the train had died with the sixty-eight victims.

Investigators found that the suitcase bomb attack was carried out by at least five people. The police soon released sketches of two suspects believed to have planted the bombs. Both appeared to have left the train just fifteen minutes before the explosions. According to the description, one of them was plump and in his thirties, while the other one had a moustache and dark skin and looked to be in his twenties. Both wore a scarf around their heads and communicated in Hindi.

In early March, the Haryana police arrested two men from Indore for allegedly selling the suitcases used in the bombings. But since they could not glean any more information from them, they were discharged in the case.

A probe conducted by the commissioner of railway safety officially determined that the explosions and fire on the Samjhauta Express had been caused by bombs placed on the upper racks of coaches GS 03431 and GS 14857. The probe also showed that the train slowed down to a speed of 20 kilometres per hour just before it was to pass through Diwana station. It seemed likely that the suspects jumped off the train at this point.

As leads dried up, investigators made no major progress in the case until the end of March. While no organization had claimed responsibility for the blasts, the police assumed it was the job of a terrorist organization and rounded up several suspects. Some were detained, while others let off after questioning. It began to appear that the LeT may have been involved, but beyond that, the investigations failed to yield any concrete results.

Meanwhile, the governments of India and Pakistan agreed to a bilateral pact to extend the passenger train and freight services between the two countries until 2010. By April, the two governments also initiated steps to increase safety and security measures on the Samjhauta Express. They started sharing information regarding the passengers travelling on the train. The peace train was back on track, exhibiting some of the interest it had attracted when it made its first cross-border journey. But the identity of the perpetrators of the February 2007 attack remained a mystery.

Then, in November 2008, more than a year after the attack, Indian investigators stumbled upon the alleged role of an Indian army officer, who was a member of the Hindu nationalist group Abhinav Bharat, in the attack. The accused, Lieutenant Colonel Shrikant Prasad Purohit, claimed that he had actually infiltrated Abhinav Bharat and was only doing his job as a military intelligence officer. In an army court of inquiry, fifty-nine people testified in his favour, saying he was collecting information on terrorists and that he was doing his job by infiltrating extremist organizations.

In October 2010, an 806-page charge sheet, prepared by the Rajasthan ATS, stated that the Samjhauta Express had been discussed as a potential target for an attack at a meeting of Hindutva groups as far back as February 2006.

It was almost serendipitous that investigators probing multiple cases across state borders connected the dots through a complex web of clues. Not long before the Samjhauta blasts, on 8 September 2006, at 1.30 p.m., four bombs had exploded in the communally sensitive town of Malegaon in Maharashtra. On 29 September 2008, another blast rocked Malegaon; this one killed four people and injured seventy-nine.

The Maharashtra ATS probe in the Malegaon 2006 serial blasts case had led the investigators to SIMI's doorstep. The ATS arrested Mohammed Ali and Asif Khan, already accused in the 7/11 Mumbai serial train blasts, and included them as accused in the 2006 Malegaon blasts.

In 2008, the Maharashtra ATS chief, Hemant Karkare, blew open the lid on organized Hindu terror for the first time, shocking other investigating agencies. While his predecessor, K.P. Raghuvanshi, had concentrated on Islamic terror groups, Karkare arrested eleven Hindutva radicals, including Lieutenant Colonel Purohit, then attached with the military intelligence unit in Nashik; Dayanand Pandey, a self-styled religious guru who ran an ashram named Sharda Peeth in Jammu; and Sadhvi Pragya Singh Thakur, an Akhil Bharatiya Vidyarthi Parishad leader turned ascetic.

Then, in 2010, not long after the Rajasthan ATS charge sheet's statement that Hindutva groups had considered the Samjhauta Express as a possible target since 2006, more revelations the same year sent the nation into a tizzy. *Tehelka*, a news magazine known for its investigative reportage, published a report on a confession by a man named Swami Aseemanand.

The magazine report said, 'On December 18, 2010, Swami Aseemanand, an elderly Bengali man and a key accused in the 2007 Mecca Masjid blast (in Hyderabad, Deccan) that claimed nine Muslim lives, voluntarily confessed before the metropolitan magistrate of Delhi about his involvement in a string of terror attacks. He did this in full knowledge that his confession could take him to the gallows.'

Naba Kumar Sarkar, popularly called Swami Aseemanand, a Hindutva leader and a rabid Muslim hater, was arrested in November 2010 after being on the run for two years. He was known to be very close to the RSS leadership, including former RSS chief K.S. Sudarshan, current chief Mohan Bhagwat, and politicians like the then Gujarat chief minister Narendra Modi and Madhya Pradesh chief minister Shivraj Singh Chauhan.

According to Aseemanand's statement, as reported by *Tehelka*, it was a momentous emotional transformation that prompted him to seek penance through a confession. According to the magazine, he told the magistrate, 'When I was lodged in the Chanchalguda district jail in Hyderabad, one of my co-inmates was Kaleem. During my interaction with Kaleem, I learnt that he was previously arrested in the Mecca Masjid bomb blast case and had to spend about a year and a half in prison. During my stay in jail, he helped me a lot and used to serve me by bringing water, food, etc. for me. I was very moved by Kaleem's good conduct and my conscience asked me to do *prayshchit* (atonement) by making a confessional statement so that the real culprits can be punished and no innocent has to suffer.'

Aseemanand declared he would spill the beans on the involvement of Hindutva leaders, including himself, in planning and executing the series of gruesome terror attacks in Malegaon in 2006 and 2008, the Samjhauta Express attack, the terror strikes at Ajmer Sharif and the Mecca Masjid, all in 2007. In a forty-two-page statement signed in Hindi, Aseemanand detailed the functioning of a Hindutva terror network and also how an RSS national executive member, Indresh Kumar, had engineered the blasts.

Kumar reportedly met Aseemanand sometime in 2005 in Gujarat and told him that the terror strikes were not his job any more and that he should focus on tribal welfare. Kumar also told him that Sunil Joshi had been appointed for the terror attacks. The finances for the attacks came from Kumar and Joshi passed it down to the men who were used for the job, according to Aseemanand's confessional statement.

As information on the involvement of RSS *pracharaks* in the Mecca Masjid and Ajmer blasts grew with every new arrest, Aseemanand's confession became the first direct evidence of the role of Hindutva terrorists in the 2006 Malegaon blasts and the Samjhauta Express blasts. The evidence pieced together by the Central Bureau of Investigation (CBI) shows that the broad terror conspiracy to target Muslims and their places of religious worship was hatched around 2001.

Three RSS pracharaks from Madhya Pradesh were apparently at the core of this conspiracy: Sunil Joshi, Ramchandra Kalsangra and Sandeep Dange.

Aseemanand's statement said that as the three became more audacious in their terror ambitions, they began to induct like-minded Hindutva radicals from other states, mainly Maharashtra, Gujarat and Rajasthan, into their terror outfit. While the new entrants were mostly from the RSS, Bajrang Dal and Vishva Hindu Parishad, some members of fringe saffron groups such as the Abhinav Bharat, Jai Vande Matram and Vanvasi Kalyan Ashram also joined the fray.

Aseemanand, who ran a Vanvasi Kalyan Ashram in the Dangs district in Gujarat, had first met Joshi in 2003. Three years after their first meeting, they became closely involved in a terror plot, according to investigators.

The flood of new information emerging from Aseemanand's statement was critical for the Maharashtra ATS. In a twist of fate, Karkare had been killed in the 26/11 terror attacks in 2008; his departure immediately impacted investigations into the Hindu terror network. As the mantle of the ATS leadership was passed back to Raghuvanshi, Kalsangra and Dange remained on the run.

In May 2010, the investigation into Hindu terror picked up pace again with the arrest of two RSS pracharaks, Devendra Gupta and Lokesh Sharma, by the Rajasthan ATS probing the Ajmer Sharif blast case.

Gupta was the RSS *vibhagpracharak* of Muzaffarnagar, Bihar. He allegedly provided logistical support to Joshi, Kalsangra and Dange, and harboured the latter two in RSS offices while they were on the run. Sharma was an RSS worker who was close to Joshi and had purchased the two Nokia cell phones that were used to trigger the bombs at the Mecca Masjid and Ajmer Sharif attack sites.

A joint investigation by the Rajasthan ATS and CBI revealed that with the exception of Sadhvi Pragya Singh Thakur, all those arrested by the Maharashtra ATS in 2008 were actually fringe players; the core group comprising Kumar,

Kalsangra and Dange allegedly held the key to the full terror plot.

In June 2010, the CBI examined a witness named Bharat Riteshwar, a resident of Valsad district in Gujarat and a close associate of Aseemanand. Riteshwar told the CBI that Joshi was a protégé of Kumar, and had his approval and logistical support for carrying out terror attacks. On 19 November 2010, the CBI cracked down on a hideout in Haridwar and arrested Aseemanand, who had been a fugitive for over two years then.

Aseemanand told the investigators that it was the heinous massacre of Hindu devotees at the Akshardham temple by Islamist suicide bombers in 2002 that had set off the first trigger for revenge. Later, the terror attack on the Sankat Mochan temple in Varanasi in March 2006 reiterated his resolve. Aseemanand gave Rs 25,000 to Joshi to arrange for the necessary logistics for the blasts. He also sent Joshi and Riteshwar to Gorakhpur to seek assistance from the rabble-rousing BJP MP Yogi Adityanath. In April 2006, Joshi held a secret meeting with Adityanath, infamous for his rabid anti-Muslim speeches. But Aseemanand told the investigators, 'Joshi came back and told me that Adityanath was not of much help.' Nevertheless, Aseemanand still went ahead with his plans, he told the magistrate.

In June 2006, Aseemanand, Riteshwar, Sadhvi Pragya and Joshi met again at Riteshwar's house in Valsad. It proved to be an important meeting, with far-reaching consequences. Joshi, for the first time, brought four associates with him—Dange, Kalsangra, Sharma and Ashok alias Amit. Aseemanand told his team, 'I told everybody that bomb *ka jawab* bomb *se dena chahiye* (I told everyone we should answer bombs with bombs).' He also suggested that Malegaon, with its majority Muslim population, should be the first target.

Aseemanand reasoned that during Partition, the Nizam of Hyderabad had wanted to secede from India, making the city a fair target for terror as well. He also suggested bombing the Ajmer Sharif Dargah as many Hindus flock there. This would deter Hindus from visiting the Sufi shrine. Another target on his list was the Aligarh Muslim University. While everyone agreed with his targets, Joshi was convinced that the Samjhauta Express should be bombed, as many Pakistanis travelled on this train.

They didn't know it then, but as the Hindu extremists busied themselves with the task of arranging for explosives and logistics, the cycle of retaliation had inched forward elsewhere—with plans being hatched to attack Mumbai's lifeline. And with that the wheels of the inexorable retributive cycle of violence wouldn't stop turning.

Matunga blast: This blast occurred at 6.24 p.m. in a Virar-bound fast train.
The first-class compartment's eastern side was completely destroyed.
The blast killed twenty-eight people and left 122 injured.

Mira Road blast: Cops cordon off the area after the first-class compartment
of the Virar fast train blew up between Mira Road and Bhayandar
at 6.23 p.m. By this time, commuters and bystanders had
managed to take all the bodies away.

Commuters pay their respects to those who lost their lives
in the 11 July 2006 carnage on an anniversary of the blast.

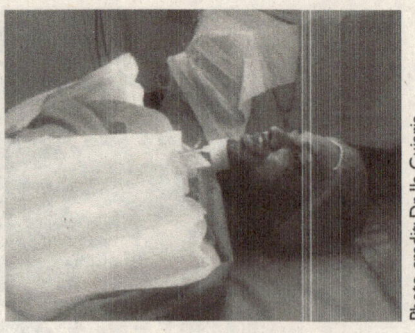

Prashant Rathi and his wife: They belong to the 'miracle family'—four members of the same family were in three different bomb-laden trains, and all of them survived.

Ashwin Boricha: The former advertising professional in Bombay Hospital's operation theatre, during one of his many eye surgeries.

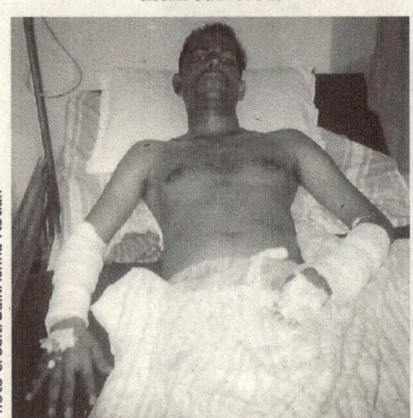

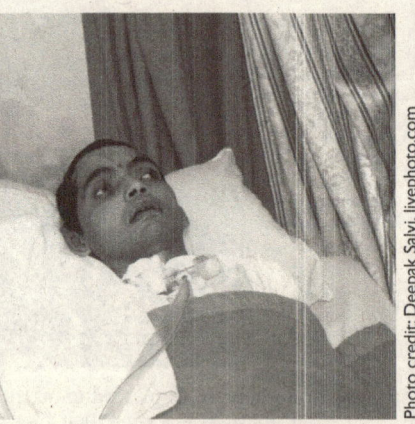

Balkrishna Kotian: The dental technician suffered several injuries on his hands and head. His eardrums were damaged in the blast and he now suffers from partial deafness.

Parag Sawant: Despite sustaining serious injuries, he battled to survive for four years. He finally succumbed to his wounds in 2010.

Chirag Chauhan: The chartered accountant and his mother, Anjana, at their residence in Andheri.

Photo credit: Deepak Salvi, livephoto.com

The accused being escorted to the special MCOCA court on the day of the verdict. At the time of their arrests, they had alleged defamation, and the media was restrained from publishing their photographs. Nine years later, still claiming they were innocent, they walked into court with their heads held high, ensuring their photos were taken.

Photo credit: Abdul Wahideen Mohammad Shaikh

Abdul Wahideen Mohammad Shaikh: An assistant teacher with Anjuman-i-Islam A.S.S. School near Grant Road in south Mumbai, he is the only man to walk free after the verdict in 2015.

Asif Bashir Khan (left) and Ehtesham Siddiqui (right) being escorted into court for the final verdict in September 2015. Asif is a civil engineer from Jalgaon and Ehtesham is a publisher from Azamgarh. Both held key positions in the SIMI leadership and have been convicted of planting a bomb each.

Tafheem Akmal Hashmi, formerly a part of the Pakistan Army, had joined the terror outfit Al-Badr, headquartered in Muzaffarabad in Pakistan-occupied Kashmir. While Tafheem was initially arrested in the case, he was discharged before the trial could begin.

Faisal Atta-ur Rahman Shaikh: The western India commander of the Lashkar-e-Taiba, in custody of the Anti-Terrorism Squad in 2006.

Sajid Marghoob Ansari: A diploma holder in industrial electronic engineering, he owned a small mobile-repair shop in Mavali, and also conducted classes on computer and mobile phone repairs. He has been convicted of helping the Pakistanis make the bombs.

Muzzammil Atta-ur Rahman Shaikh: Faisal's youngest brother, he worked at Data Core Technologies prior to his arrest. He has been convicted of providing logistical support to those members of the group who trained in Pakistan.

Naved Hussain Khan: He worked as a floor manager in RSR Sales Services, in Secunderabad, before his arrest. He has been convicted of planting one of the bombs.

Mohammed Majid Shafi on his way to court for the verdict in September 2015.

Kamal Ansari being escorted to court for the verdict in September 2015. Kamal hails from Basupatti, a tiny village in Bihar, close to the India–Nepal border. He has been convicted of planting one of the bombs.

Mohammed Ali Alam Shaikh being escorted for the verdict in September 2015. He used to sell *tilasmi moti* and was a SIMI activist. The bombs were made in his Govandi shanty.

Dr Tanveer Ansari being escorted to court for the verdict in September 2015. Prior to his arrest, Tanveer was working as a medical registrar at M.H. Saboo Siddique Maternity and General Hospital in south Mumbai.

Photo credit: National Investigating Agency's website

Hafeez Saeed: The amir of the Jama'at-ud-Da'wah, a terrorist organization based in Pakistan, comprising people belonging to the Ahl-e-Hadith sect of Islam. The Lashkar-e-Taiba is the armed wing of the JuD.

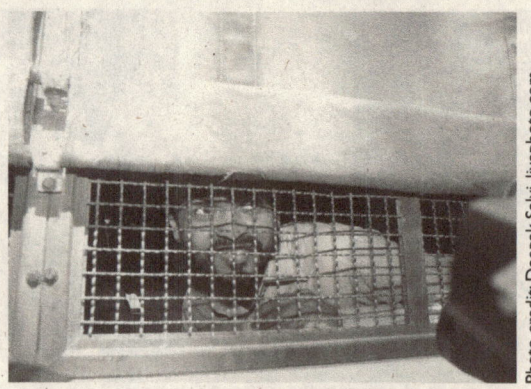

Photo credit: Deepak Salvi, livephoto.com

Zameer Latifur Rehman Shaikh: A taxi driver, Zameer being escorted to court for the verdict in September 2015.

Photo credit: Deepak Salvi, livephoto.com

Suhail Mehmood Shaikh: The 'spiritual healer' being escorted to court for the verdict in September 2015.

Zaki-ur-Rehman Lakhvi: Co-founder of the Lashkar-e-Taiba, he is also its chief military commander.

Photo credit: Tariq Khan

Police Inspector Bhimdev Rathod: He was attached to the Anti-Terrorism Squad.

Photo credit: Sheela Thakare

Special Public Prosecutor Raja Thakare: He examined 192 witnesses during the course of the trial. He defended several high-profile accused before choosing to represent the investigating agency.

Photo credit: Deepak Salvi, livephoto.com

Krish Pal Raghuvanshi (centre) with Vasant Tajne (third from left).

Photo credit: Western Railway Archives

The Churchgate railway station in 2006.
The bomb planters got into the seven local trains from here.

Yug Mohit Chaudhry: The defence counsel for seven of the thirteen accused. He is a human rights lawyer and a well-known crusader against the death penalty.

Prakash Shetty: The noted criminal lawyer defended four of the accused, including Faisal Atta-ur Rahman Shaikh, and is currently on the panel of lawyers representing the National Investigating Agency.

Sharif Shaikh: He is on the panel of lawyers appointed by the Jamiat-Ulama-e-Maharashtra and defended two of the accused in the case, Ehtesham Siddiqui and Majid Shafi.

Wahab Khan: He is on the panel of lawyers appointed by Jamiat-Ulama-e-Maharashtra and defended five of the accused in the case, including Dr Tanveer Ansari and Asif Bashir Khan.

13

The Courtroom Cast

Heads turned as a young man wearing sleek black pants and a crisp black coat walked down the corridors of the Mumbai City Civil and Sessions Court. Twenty-nine-year-old Shahid Azmi's mother, Rehana Azmi, would lovingly call him Fardeen Khan, after the Bollywood actor known for his boyish looks and inimitable style. Shahid was a rookie, but no one was surprised when he decided to defend Faisal, Muzzammil, Naved and Zameer in the 7/11 blasts case. Soft-spoken, but wildly passionate about his work, Shahid was a lethal combination. After all, he had been to hell and back.

Disillusioned after the 1992 riots, Shahid joined the Jammu Kashmir Liberation Front, a militant organization based in the Valley. In only a few months, the fifteen-year-old returned to his mother and three brothers, to their home in Govandi, one of the largest Muslim pockets in Mumbai. Shahid often admitted that he 'couldn't be a radical'. But his past followed him to Mumbai. The police detained him and charged him with several sections under the stringent TADA in 1994. Just like under the MCOCA, a confession under TADA could be used against him. Incorrect entries in the police files showed that the teenager had been apprehended from a Delhi market three days after he was actually detained in Mumbai. Shahid was accused of conspiring to murder Jammu and Kashmir political leader Dr Farooq Abdullah and was imprisoned for five years.

In his time at Tihar Jail, a maximum security prison in Delhi, Shahid continued his college education from Indira Gandhi National Open University (IGNOU), a distance learning university that has long been a haven for many prisoners hoping to reintegrate into mainstream society after they are released from prison. Although Shahid had been convicted by the special TADA court, his sentence was overturned by the Supreme Court a year later as the police had no evidence but a 'confession' against him.

Shahid's tryst with the law did not end there. After his release, he simultaneously completed a course in journalism and a degree in law from Kishinchand Chellaram College in Mumbai. At university, Shahid spoke with a slight stammer, talking only when spoken to.

As a lawyer, he saw every client as a victim of a communalized police force. He paid the police back for what he had gone through; he broke down every case to the minutest of details, astonishing everyone with his grasp of the art of cross-examination.

As Shahid's reputation in the courts grew, his family moved from Govandi to a more respectable address at Taximen's Colony in Kurla, near his new office. Shahid's success was becoming apparent. He worked on cases until late in the night, and helped free more and more people who had been held under the now repealed Prevention of Terrorism Act (POTA). By 2006, Shahid had more cases than he could handle. His practice had been a massive setback for the Mumbai Police, who often tried brushing the errors in their investigation under the carpet, aided by incompetent lawyers representing the accused, especially in terror-related cases.

However, Shahid's past never left him. *Tehelka* reported how a few years ago, in a heated moment, Shahid argued in a court that even Lord Ram had waged violence to secure justice. The media screamed blue murder. A police case was registered. The judge called in Shahid for a chat. 'But it's true,' he insisted when the judge cautioned that there were rumours he had been convicted for terrorism. 'I wear that conviction as a badge of honour.' The judge told the police he never heard Shahid speak of Lord Ram and the case collapsed.

~

On 9 October 2006, just days after eleven of the thirteen accused 'confessed' to their roles in the train blasts, their statements fell, one after the other, like a house of cards. The accused alleged torture and wanted to retract their confessions. It had been two and a half months since the arrests of Kamal, Faisal and Tanveer. When the black veils were lifted for identification, their faces looked gaunt and pale. It was unclear when they had last had a full night's sleep.

Shahid looked at these men and recalled all the torture he had undergone as a minor in the interrogation room. He saw himself in every man detained on terror allegations. Illegal detention and torture under the pretence of inquiry was commonplace. Their best years will be destroyed in jails and they will bear the brunt of the case, despite being innocent, he thought to himself. He later articulated this to the media in his interviews.

Maharashtra is ranked the no. 1 state when it comes to custodial torture and deaths across India. Since Shahid's release from Tihar until 2003, 128 custodial deaths had been recorded in the state. So when Zameer, Kamal, Faisal, Muzzammil, Ehtesham, Tanveer and Suhail raised the issue of custodial torture and forced signatures on the confessional statements, Shahid insisted that their pleas be heard by the court. At Shahid's behest, instead of ordering the seven of them to file applications, Special Judge Mridula Bhatkar noted their complaints. At this point, he hadn't even filed an application to represent all of them and yet, he already spoke for them all. A formal application to withdraw the confessional statements was made one month later, in November. 'I signed because they threatened to implicate me in the Malegaon case as well,' wrote Mohammed Ali, in whose shanty in Govandi the bombs were made. This was right before his actual arrest in the Malegaon case.

Nine days after the oral complaints of the accused were recorded by the court, 'deshbhakts', acting as stooges of the Mumbai Police, staged protests. Why had Shahid Azmi taken up the cases of these men, they questioned, never satisfied by his answers. Shahid believed that young Muslim boys, from slum pockets with large Muslim populations, were caught in a vicious cycle of terror. Using instruments like confessions, the police would pick them up from their homes, put them behind bars and charge them under stringent laws like the MCOCA and the UAPA. Eventually, some turned to terror activities as a form of dissent.

In cases like these, it was difficult for the accused to make their voices heard. Often they were forced to resort to subpar legal aid as few had the money to find a lawyer to represent them. With the accused on legal aid, police agencies got terrific conviction rates. Until Shahid, and a few others who were willing to stick their neck out for these men, came along. He had become a force to reckon with.

Seated in his office one evening in October 2006, Shahid received a phone call from someone who identified himself as Ravi Pujari, a self-proclaimed patriotic ganglord. He had an ultimatum for Shahid. 'Withdraw the *vakalatnama* in the 7/11 case within seventy-two hours. We know everything, where you go and where you stay, even the food you eat. It won't take us much time to squeeze the life out of you.' Before he could even think of a reply, the line went silent. Shahid refused to bow down. The next day he wrote a letter to the Kurla police station, reporting the phone call, filed an application about the threat in the special court, and then continued his work— filing an application in one case and cross-examining a witness in another.

'Threats given to advocates appearing before this court are contempt of the advocate and thus, contempt of court,' he said before leaving the special court. Judge Bhatkar said that she would take up the issue because it was a serious matter. However, Shahid's application was promptly rejected citing the court's lack of 'jurisdiction and power' on such an issue, and it was decided that it was a matter for the police to investigate. This decision had been taken in Shahid's absence. When he read the order, he walked away with his head bowed in disappointment. The incident did not deter him and he continued to represent the accused in the 7/11 case.

Shahid knew what he was up against in court. The ATS had put their best foot forward. Shahid would have to face someone far older, sharper and more experienced—Special Public Prosecutor Raja Thakare. Tall, fair-skinned and balding, Thakare came from a family of intellectuals, doctors and engineers. Shahid's five years of experience dimmed before a formidable Thakare, who had a three-decade-old practice. Halfway through his career, after representing much of Mumbai's underworld, including gangsters like Chhota Rajan and Dawood Ibrahim, Thakare switched from the dark side. He became a special public prosecutor for the CBI in the 1992 securities scam involving Harshad Mehta. Thakare's expertise in breaking down and making sense of complex paperwork had made him an instant hit with the agencies. His background as a defence lawyer enabled him to think like his opponents. He also kept away from the media and barely flashed his white teeth for the cameras. Working with government agencies had made Thakare realize how excited they would get after cracking a case, so much so that they would completely forget to tie up loose ends in the investigation. He was a stickler for the law and faithful to the people he represented. He denied any mistakes by the investigation team, even though such mistakes were what he feared the most while representing them in a court.

In 2006, Thakare was on a high after successfully representing the CBI in the multi-crore stamp paper scam against Abdul Karim Telgi. Rumours that the 7/11 blasts case would be offered to him had spread beyond the stinking ground-floor canteen in the heritage City Civil and Sessions Court building and the 100-year-old court library. When the officers approached him, he readily accepted the case.

Thakare would never forget the day some of the accused were brought to the Sewree Court for the first time after their arrests—much before they had been charged under the stringent MCOCA sections. The courtroom and the corridors were filled with bearded men and burqa-clad women, and, for the first time in his life, Thakare felt the strength of a community.

Thakare moved quickly. Under the Indian Penal Code, an accused can be kept in police custody for only fourteen days. Because the officers needed time to investigate, the police first took them into custody in six of the seven cases registered one by one, after which the MCOCA was applied and their confessions were recorded.

During those days, narco-analysis (which limits a person's imagination, making it difficult to lie) was something investigators often resorted to. The technique was used to fill in missing links in several cases and this case was no exception. Permission for the tests was granted every single time. A few days before Shahid was threatened, Thakare filed a request for narco-analysis, brain-mapping and polygraph tests to be conducted on a few of the accused. For these tests, the consent of the accused did not matter. The examination was conducted by a Dr Malini Iyer at the Forensic Science Laboratory (FSL) in Bangalore.

In many of these tests, sodium pentothal would be used in excess, causing the men to fall unconscious, have severe headaches, stomach pain, nausea and weakness. In some cases, their vital signs would become weak during the process. In 2010, this test was finally ruled unconstitutional by the Supreme Court, which held that a man cannot be forced to implicate himself without his free will. Dr Iyer later faced criminal charges for allegedly forging her educational qualifications to obtain a job at FSL, Bangalore. She was reinstated in 2013 by a High Court order. Interestingly enough, the statements of most of the crucial witnesses, including eyewitnesses at the railway station and the conspiracy meetings, were recorded after the narco-analysis test.

On 30 November 2006, two constables carried the 10,667-page charge sheet, in twenty-six volumes, packed in aluminium trunks, to the special court.

When a defence lawyer is appointed, he bills the accused based on the number of pages filed in the charge sheet against him by the investigating officer, among other things. It was evident that the lawyers would need time to go through this particular document. In this case, time was on the side of the accused as the court was occupied with other cases. Delays in Indian courts notoriously surpass delays in any court worldwide. The trial wasn't scheduled until June 2007.

During this time, Shahid became a pillar of support for all of the accused, even though he only represented Faisal, Muzzammil, Naved and Zameer.

That year, section 2(1)(e) of the MCOCA was applied for the first time in three cases—the 7/11 case, the Malegaon blasts case and the Aurangabad arms haul case. This section charged perpetrators with the formation of an organized crime syndicate to 'promote insurgency'. Shahid had sleepless nights trying to understand a technical point in this clause. How could the clause of insurgency, which is constitutionally a matter under only the Central government, be used by the state to charge suspects? According to Shahid, the term had become repugnant as the UAPA already dealt with insurgency in great detail.

He would challenge this section in the law, he announced to the men he represented. Shahid, with the help of another lawyer P.A. Sebastian, prepared a bulky petition and filed it in the Bombay High Court in July 2008. The entire process had, so far, cost the accused approximately Rs 3 lakh, and this included the meagre fees they paid Shahid. There was no way they would be able to afford a prolonged court battle.

So Shahid took it upon himself to ensure he saw the case through.

Shahid had already spoken to the famous Supreme Court lawyer Shanti Bhushan, who believed there was merit in his contention. But these efforts were in vain; even if these men managed to scrape together the costs for a Supreme Court case, they would never be able to afford a lawyer good enough to defend them.

Shahid also needed more time to prepare their defence. Despite lapses in the investigation, he knew that it would be tough to save these men from the gallows. The charge sheet filed in court was a truncated copy, with the names and addresses of the witnesses hidden using white ink. This was of no help if Shahid wanted to investigate the witnesses independently.

Shahid strategized on how he could raise enough funds to take the battle to the Supreme Court. He himself did not have enough money for such a colossal legal proceeding. He decided to involve charitable organizations to support him.

~

Situated in the heart of a south Mumbai locality largely populated by Muslims, in Bhendi Bazaar, was the office of the Jamiat-Ulama-e-Maharashtra. It had been known to help riot victims receive the compensation they were entitled to. The organization was a branch of the Jamiat-Ulama-e-Hind, a trust founded in 1919 to help war-affected Muslims from Turkey, with the focus later shifting to victims of natural calamities. Later, the group helped those affected by the Partition. The group had also provided monetary aid to Muslims affected by the 1968 Ahmedabad riots and the 2006 Malegaon blasts. Until 2003, when Shahid began his practice, the

Jamiat-Ulama-e-Hind was one of the few organizations providing such a service.

In 2005, Shahid came in contact with the Jamiat-Ulama-e-Hind. He was representing the general secretary Gulzar Azmi's two sons in an MCOCA case. 'There is a group of young men who desperately need aid,' Shahid told Azmi. 'They are victims of police atrocities and nothing else. I don't need to tell you, you know everything,' Shahid said, referring to Azmi's two sons, Abrar and Anwar, who were accused of using the name of their school friend (whom they hadn't met in twenty years) and Chhota Shakeel's right-hand man, Faheem Machmach, to threaten two women. The evidence against the two boys was flimsy, but they were unable to get bail for a couple of months because of the draconian MCOCA. Shahid and Azmi spoke at length about the accused in all the three cases Shahid was handling—the 7/11 blasts case, the Aurangabad arms haul and the 2006 Malegaon blasts.

Shahid's proposal to the Jamiat-Ulama-e-Hind was clear: Jamiat funds should be used to file the Supreme Court appeal. This idea appealed to Gulzar Azmi, who was in his seventies then and frustrated with the misuse of MCOCA. He agreed to take Shahid's proposal forward. A few days later, the Jamiat received a letter from the accused in prison, quoting the word *riqab* from the Quran, with the request to provide them with legal aid. Riqab signifies the giving of money to slaves in a bid to buy their freedom. Further, a Hadith also states that for every limb of the servant freed, Allah frees a limb of the one who freed him from slavery. Thus, the reward is equitable to the deed.

Shahid didn't stop at convincing Azmi. He met the interim president of the Jamiat-Ulama-e-Hind, Maulana Sayyed Arshad Madani, along with the relatives of the accused.

Madani was impressed, and offered to help Shahid from the zakat (charity to take care of the needs of the poor, considered compulsory by some Muslims) Jamiat received from families.

A dedicated legal aid committee was formed by the Jamiat, with Azmi at the helm and Shahid as its public face. This cell spent Rs 8 lakh in the first quarter of 2008 to cover the legal costs of the 7/11 MCOCA petition. Still, this covered only the expenses for getting the petition admitted in the Supreme Court for a detailed hearing. Paying for well-known experts, like Shanti Bhushan, Nitya Kumar Jain and Nitya Ramakrishnan, would cost Rs 10–25 lakh each, even if the lawyers accepted a reduced fees. Yet, the monetary support received by the organization for this cause was overwhelming. Even after bearing the entire bill for the Supreme Court appeal, the Jamiat was still left with substantial funds.

Shahid Azmi never asked for a penny and accepted whatever he was given for all the cases he handled on Jamiat's behalf. Through the Jamiat, he also represented the co-founder of the IM, Sadiq Israr Shaikh, in 2008.

Gulzar Azmi wondered what the organization could do with the funds. Madani's answer was simple. 'The money has come in their name, let it be used for their cause,' he told Azmi over the phone. The Jamiat went on to cover the legal expenses of the entire 7/11 trial.

The legal aid cell lived on after the trial. Today, the fund provides 90 per cent of all legal aid to Muslim youth accused of terrorism. They base their funding decision on a screening process that helps ascertain, to some degree, whether a person is innocent or not.

14

Trial Interrupted

7 August 2007

The last six months of 2007 were unlike any other time in the history of Sessions Court no. 57. The courtroom resembled a tiny battlefield. This was before the Jamiat-Ulama-e-Maharashtra stepped in. Each day, an agitated yet determined group of around seven or eight people would parade into the courtroom, handkerchiefs emblazoned with the words 'No Faith' covering a part of their faces. 'No faith in Judge Mridula Bhatkar,' said the pieces of paper some of them carried in their pockets.

'We are cancelling the vakalatnama of all our advocates. We do not want to proceed with this case as we have no faith in the judge,' Asif said coolly, as he protested the judge's decisions in the case. Judge Bhatkar, however, remained unmoved. 'Why don't you approach the right authority?' she asked. This was not the first time the judge had witnessed such behaviour against her. The other accused in the case—Kamal, Ehtesham, Tanveer and Abdul Wahid—had acted similarly in the past.

It had all started when the men realized that the trial in the short and stern MCOCA judge Mridula Bhatkar's court would go on with or without their cooperation.

The accused had tried using several tactics to delay the case. Some of them refused to appoint lawyers to represent them, hiring and firing several lawyers, or citing lack of funds as the reason for not hiring a lawyer. But when the judge did not relent and gave them one last opportunity to hire a lawyer or accept legal aid, all of them, except Abdul Wahid, hired one. Abdul Wahid appealed to the court with the names of several prominent lawyers, including that of Rizwan Merchant, a noted criminal lawyer representing several high-profile accused involved in MCOCA cases. The judge called Merchant and asked him if he was ready to argue the charges. 'How will I prepare an argument [on the charges] in a day?' Merchant asked the judge. 'You have two days, Mr Merchant, I am sure it is possible,' she smiled. Left with little choice, he agreed.

Rizwan Merchant became an amicus curiae, or friend of the court, and advised Judge Bhatkar on the case thereafter. Since the assistance required at this point was defending the charges against Abdul Wahid, Merchant did that as well. It was only much later that Abdul Wahid got his own lawyer.

On 7 August 2007, Judge Bhatkar asked the court interpreter to read out the charges against the thirteen men standing in a row in front of her. In a criminal case, arguments on the charges levelled by the prosecution and the subsequent framing of charges marks the beginning of a trial, and sets the charges that are levelled against the accused.

The men were now convinced that the judge would not delay the trial. In the absence of an order to stay the trial, Asif devised another solution to buy time and prepare their defence—ask for the case to be transferred to another court.

After hearing the arguments of the prosecution and the defence, Judge Bhatkar concluded that the accused would be tried for several sections under the Indian Penal Code and the MCOCA, pertaining to criminal conspiracy, forming and abetting an organized crime syndicate and causing death, and harbouring members of an organized crime syndicate.

That day in court, Asif looked at Abdul Wahid, with an application clutched tightly in his fist, and pushed it forward towards the judge. The application said that they had 'no faith in the court' and wanted the case to be transferred to another court. Judge Bhatkar continued to carefully tick the twenty-nine charges that had already been read out, and said that they should approach the right authority for a change of court.

'These are serious offences. We have been framed because the ATS did not get the real accused. Give us a month's time to explain all this,' Asif urged. One by one, they were all called to the witness box and were asked if they pleaded guilty and if not, the trial could begin against them. 'I am not guilty,' Kamal said in Hindi. Then came Tanveer, 'I refuse the charge, I have no faith in this court'. 'I am innocent,' echoed Faisal, who came to the witness box next, as did Mohammed Ali. 'I refuse to participate in the legal proceedings,' Ehtesham said with conviction. 'I don't have faith in this court, so I don't want to say anything,' Sajid said, as did his brother-in-law Abdul Wahid. The rest of them—Muzzammil, Suhail, Naved and Asif—repeated 'no faith'.

The reason Majid gave the court was innovative. He said that an Urdu translator should be used as he did not understand Hindi. In six months, Majid had never made any such statement before. He admitted it was Shahid's idea when Judge Bhatkar probed. However, Majid made his request in

Hindi. 'The accused no. 5 has been conversing in Hindi and understands Hindi, so there is no need for an interpreter,' she noted. An accused is supposed to sign on a copy of the charges against him. But none of them, except Zameer, signed the papers.

Judge Bhatkar asked Merchant his opinion on the correct procedure when the accused refused to cooperate on such an occasion. 'Under section 230 of the Criminal Procedure Code, if the accused does not wish to plead (guilty or not), the judge can go ahead with the examination of witnesses,' Merchant said.

Nonetheless, Judge Bhatkar granted the accused a month's time to institute procedures to get the court changed, but even by the end of the year, neither the Supreme Court nor the Bombay High Court stayed the trial. Whenever the accused asked for extra time, Special Public Prosecutor Raja Thakare vehemently objected. 'This is not the way an accused can behave inside a courtroom. The court does not need their permission to conduct proceedings. They have been given enough and more chances,' he declared.

The battle in court continued between the stubborn group insistent on buying more time, as the noose gradually tightened around their necks, and a judge who refused to work according to the whims of others, in the months to come.

One September afternoon, the accused were angrier than usual. Judge Bhatkar had agreed to forward their 'transfer of court' applications to the principal judge of the Sessions Court, but was yet to act on it. Judge Bhatkar justified the delay by saying there were conflicting opinions about whom the papers should go to. '*Agar aapko itna kanoon samajhta nahi, toh aap idhar kyun baithi hain?* (If you don't understand this much legality, why are you occupying that chair?)' Ehtesham and

Abdul Wahid shot back at her. 'You cannot conduct a trial against us.'

That day, the judge simply sent them back to their cells and made note of this behaviour.

~

The non-cooperation did not happen overnight. The accused arrested by the ATS that year in the three cases—Aurangabad, 7/11 and Malegaon—were lodged in the high-security Anda cell. The name of this particular cell is conceived from the way it is shaped—literally like an egg. The enclosure had five barracks and an open area at the centre. Each barrack had three 10-foot cells and a tiny space leading up to it. There were three inmates in each cell, which gave them just about enough space to sleep. The Anda cell also housed undertrials from the don Chhota Rajan's gang, who were known as the Nana Company. Accused from the dreaded don Dawood's gang were referred to as the D Company. In the same way, the accused in the 7/11 serial blasts, the Malegaon blasts and the Aurangabad arms haul case were called the ATS Company, as they had been arrested by the ATS.

The cells were opened at 6 a.m. every day when the inmates would be allowed to come out to the space outside their cells but would still be imprisoned by the barrack gates. The ATS Company would assemble each day to discuss their case and the importance of preparing a good defence. They shared a common complaint that the orders were never in their favour. 'Sajid was brutally tortured; everyone saw his wounds but what happened? Nothing. We have complained against the ATS officers entering Arthur Road Jail, forcing us to become approvers, but no action has been taken against them. Our complaints against jail officials are all in the cold storage . . .' they would repeat over and over again.

~

It was December 2007 when the first witness was examined in the case. Prakash Shetty, more experienced and older than Shahid Azmi, now represented Faisal, Naved, Kamal and Zameer. When asked if the men wanted to cross-examine the witness since thirteen of them had boycotted the trial, all of them again held up pieces of paper stating they had no faith in the court, and that their trial be transferred to another court. The judge, however, observed that the accused were not ready to defend themselves by using their constitutional rights. The court's duty is to give a fair trial to the victims as well as the accused, the accused replied. But the judge cut them off midway, 'This place is not for making speeches.'

Instead of any other lawyer, Merchant, amicus curiae in the case, cross-examined Nagesh Baburao Dhone, a sub-inspector, and witness number 1 in the trial. In the course of the trial, 192 prosecution witnesses were examined. A week after the first cross-examination, Judge Bhatkar was transferred as principal judge to Kolhapur, along with two other judges, who were also promoted.

Three months later, the Supreme Court stayed the court proceedings in the train blasts case, pending further orders as it admitted the petition challenging the MCOCA's insurgency-related section. The thirteen men never misbehaved in court again. It would be months before the trial would start again; the accused heaved a sigh of relief.

~

Arthur Road Jail

At 9 a.m., there was a blaring sound from a loudspeaker inside Arthur Road Jail. Thirty-seven people were asked to assemble near Lal Gate, an area inside the jail compound and what stood between the prison and the free world outside. That day, prisoners from the Aurangabad arms haul case and the 7/11 blasts case were going to be transferred to other prisons in Kolhapur, Nagpur and Ratnagiri. On Saturday, 28 June 2008, the jail authorities had requisitioned a squad from the police headquarters, after which police escorts reached the jail.

While nineteen of them gathered in the central area of the jail, Kamal and Tanveer refused to come out. 'Why should we come out? Why are we being transferred without a court order?' The men started screaming in unison. They had begun questioning all orders from the jail officials. But the Arthur Road Jail superintendent, Swati Sathe, had made up her mind. She had decided that this band of friends had to be separated and sent to different prisons. By staying their trial, the Supreme Court had given her an opportunity to do that. Arthur Road Jail is situated just a few kilometres away from the Sessions Court; but with the trial stayed, they wouldn't have to mark their presence in court. In addition, Arthur Road Jail was extremely overcrowded—2500 prisoners were kept in a jail with a capacity for 804 people.

At 11.40 a.m., the first lot of prisoners had already been sent to Ratnagiri. They had argued with the jail authorities, but Sathe had been in no mood to entertain any discussions. 'I will not allow you to go on your legs,' she had warned them. When they refused, the jail siren rang out, spelling their doom. The siren in Arthur Road Jail meant that officials could now use force to bring the 'situation under control'. The sounds of sticks and belts flaying, and the screeches of the nineteen men, haunted the prisoners in that jail for a long time to come. Kamal was beaten up in the open space meant for group activities. He told the other prisoners that Tanveer was also badly assaulted. Ehtesham started running to save his skin. But when he was pinned down, Zameer jumped on him in a bid to save him. 'No, don't hit him,' he cried, as he took the beatings on his back.

An hour later, an eerie silence descended on the jail. Tanveer leant against a wall near the main gate. He was the strongest of them all, a fitness freak, but he now looked like a wreck. Every inch of his body was sore. While being transferred, they had to be medically examined by the jail doctor as per protocol. But the doctor claimed he saw no injuries on them. Later, when the accused approached the High Court with regard to the incident, Justice Bilal Nazki called these doctors 'reprehensible' and 'shameful'. The accused were shoved into vans and sent to Nagpur, moaning in pain at the slightest of movement.

Badly beaten up and injured, Ehtesham and Abdul Wahid were the last ones in Arthur Road Jail. 'I think they have kept us back because they want to beat us up just a little more,' Ehtesham told Abdul Wahid, in his soft voice. 'I don't think so. How much more can they possibly hit us?' Abdul Wahid responded. Just then a jail official called out their names and they were sent to Kolhapur with fifteen others.

The conflict in the jail left wounds on all the accused. Tanveer's wounds remained untreated until he was examined fifteen days later. He had injuries on his forearms, shoulders, and had fractured his left elbow and a bone in his palm. Kamal was examined in Nagpur Jail on 16 July 2008, nearly twenty days after he complained of a swelling on his right thumb. He had fractured his thumb, and had sustained injuries on his left arm and chest. Ehtesham was also examined in the Government Hospital at Kolhapur, twenty days after being moved to a prison in that city. He had eleven injuries and had fractured the bones in his right palm. Asif, who was examined on 19 July 2008, had three weals, swollen red marks left behind by severe blows, and had sustained injuries to his shoulder and chest.

In Mumbai, when Shahid heard of the incident, he was furious, as was the fiery judge, Justice Bilal Nazki, of the Bombay High Court. Shahid filed a petition through Suhail's son, Saeed, on 7 July. When asked for an explanation, Sathe tried justifying the force, stating that her men were being beaten up by the inmates. She claimed they were pelting stones and bricks on jail officers, trying to release people from high-security cells. However, when the incident was probed by the principal judge of the Sessions Court, he found that the accused did not have access to bricks and that, while some amount of force was necessary, the amount used was excessive.

On 21 July 2009, a year after the incident, a division bench of justices Nazki and A.R. Joshi observed, 'Before coming to the legal submissions made, we may hold that the jail superintendent and the supporting staff used the force excessively and for reasons extraneous and not to maintain discipline in the jail. It has to be remembered that the convicts or the undertrials are human beings and they have to be treated like human beings. The jail authorities who have custody over them have the special responsibility to protect their rights and, in fact, they are their custodians, reformers and counsellors. They cannot assume the role by which they turn into villains. They, in fact, should command respect from the prisoners and that respect should come as a result of their conduct with the prisoners.'

The bench also observed that the transfers of the accused were illegal. The jail manual wasn't followed by officials even as a formality. The chief secretary of the state was directed to initiate a departmental inquiry against Sathe and her team. This was a huge setback for the state as authorities were made accountable to this extent for the first time.

Without much ado, the state appealed the decision of the High Court. On 2 November 2012, a Supreme Court bench of justices T.S. Thakur and F.M. Kalifulla called the High Court's observations 'premature' and the judicial inquiry 'preliminary' and 'flawed'. However, they also stated that the transfers were illegal.

15

'We Did It'—Indian Mujahideen

February 2009

Special Public Prosecutor Raja Thakare, who was representing the Anti-Terrorism Squad, was in his Handloom House office, a stone's throw from the iconic Chhatrapati Shivaji (Railway) Terminus. His office was opposite the Kalaigar mosque and the street was bustling with Muslims who had come to offer prayers. In stark contrast, there was complete silence inside where Thakare sat still, staring at the wall. Nobody who knew him would have made the mistake of disturbing him at this time. Thakare was representing both, the ATS, in the 7/11 train blasts case, and the Mumbai Crime Branch, in the Indian Mujahideen case. The IM case pertained to emails sent to media organizations soon after the blasts in Lucknow and Varanasi in 2007, and Rampur, Bengaluru, Ahmedabad and Delhi in 2008.

At this point, Thakare was frustrated because he was stuck between two agencies that constantly fought with one another. This animosity between the ATS and the Mumbai

Police's Crime Branch had become a public spectacle. A video recording of a police interrogation by the Crime Branch had been aired on a TV channel on 27 February 2009. Every ATS officer shared one thought: the recording had shamed them before the public. Rumour had it that the video had been leaked by the Crime Branch to embarrass their rival. It was this video that Thakare had just finished viewing.

> Atif Amin [who was killed in the 2008 Batla House encounter in Delhi] and I had made a plan at Saraimir, Azamgarh, in 2006 to plant bombs in Mumbai after the Delhi and Varanasi serial blasts in March 2006. As per the plan, I went to a village Surjanpur and met Abu Rashid and Dr Shahnawaz, and prepared them for the 7/11 Mumbai local train bomb blasts. Thereafter, I went to Mumbai to my brother's house in Cheetah Camp. Some days after I came back [to Mumbai], Abu Rashid and Dr Shahnawaz came to Mumbai. Abu Rashid took a flat on rent in Sewree, and he and Dr Shahnawaz started staying there . . . I left my house in Cheetah Camp and started staying with them. I had brought timers when I came back to Mumbai from my village. Atif came from Delhi to the Sewree flat, bringing Rs 50,000 with him. I then sent Atif to Riyaz Bhatkal [one of the founders of Indian Mujahideen] to get explosives. Atif, in turn, convinced a boy named Sajid [from Azamgarh] to help [with] the blasts.

The video was very clear. A man, visibly in police custody, with only his face and shoulders seen, probably tortured, was giving an unwavering statement. Sadiq Israr Shaikh claimed that the IM was behind every single blast in the country from 2005 to 2008. He recounted in his video confession how he, along with four others, planned and executed the 7/11 train blasts. His story didn't just vary from the charge sheet filed two and a half years ago by the ATS against thirteen men, most of them belonging to the SIMI, it painted a completely different story of the blasts, narrating how the IM, an India-based terrorist organization, led by Riyaz Bhatkal alias Riyaz Shahbandri alias Roshan Khan, was the true perpetrator of the Mumbai train blasts.

> I bought five first-class train passes for myself, Atif, the boy from Azamgarh, Sajid, Dr Shahnawaz and Abu Rashid. I obtained the timetables for Mumbai Railways and studied them . . . In the meantime, we obtained pressure cookers and travelling bags from Sewree. As per the plan, we gathered in the Sewree flat on the morning of 11 July 2006 and assembled the seven bombs there. Before that, I had taken those four men and travelled with them in first-class local trains from Churchgate. In line with the plan, I started from the Sewree flat with a bag containing a bomb; from Dadar, I went by the Western Railways to Churchgate. Atif left the flat with two bags containing bombs and I kept the bag containing the bomb in a first-class bogie . . .

What followed was a chillingly systematic description of the planting of each of the seven bombs in different Western Railway local trains. The bombs were in pressure cookers, all of them had detonators, which were attached to timers belonging to a brand called Samay. Each pressure cooker had a capacity of 5 litres. All the bombs were kept in separate travelling bags and set to go off at 6.30 p.m., during evening peak hours. Each of the bags was kept in the rack of a first-class compartment. Sadiq and Abu Rashid had disposed of the remaining raw material for the bombs in the Mahim Creek. After the blasts, Abu Rashid remained in Sewree, and Sajid in his Andheri house. While Shahnawaz travelled to Lucknow, Sadiq and Atif boarded a train to Azamgarh, two days after the blasts, on 13 July 2006.

Born in Shivaji Nagar, in Govandi's Cheetah Camp, Sadiq lived with his wife, his parents and his brother's family. Since 1996, he had worked as a refrigerator technician with Godrej at their plant in Vikhroli. After losing his job in 2000, Sadiq shifted to Saraimir, in the Azamgarh district of Uttar Pradesh, while his brother stayed on in Mumbai. Sadiq returned to Mumbai in 2006 to work with an outsourcing firm. On 23 September 2008, he was arrested by a team from the Mumbai Crime Branch, headed by Assistant Police Inspector Dinesh Kadam.

Once a SIMI member, Sadiq believed that the organization was all talk and no action. Along with Riyaz and Iqbal Bhatkal, Abdus Subhan Usman Qureshi alias Subhan Qureshi and Amir Raza Khan, he founded the IM. Sadiq trained under Azam Cheema, at an LeT terrorist training camp in Muzaffarnagar, Pakistan. He reached Pakistan via Bangladesh and sent more recruits to Pakistan for training.

By the end of 2008, the Crime Branch arrested twenty-three IM members in all. Two other arrested members—Ansar Ahmed Badshah Shaikh and Mohammed Arif Badruddin Shaikh—had also claimed that Sadiq was involved in the 7/11 train blasts case, only to retract their confessions later. Ansar said that Sadiq had initially asked him to help deliver a 'parcel' from Hyderabad, but he had refused because his wife was pregnant at the time. It was only later that Sadiq told him about his involvement in the 7/11 train blasts. Mohammed Arif, the owner of an electronic goods shop, confessed that he met Sadiq through SIMI and helped make ten timers, using

Samay watches, in February 2006. He realized later that Sadiq had been involved in the 7/11 blasts.

The IM revelations had planted a seed of doubt in the ATS's 7/11 investigations. If IM recruits were involved in the blasts, then the list of accused the ATS had created was incorrect.

During a press conference on 24 September 2008 just a day after Sadiq's arrest, Rakesh Maria, who was heading the Mumbai Police's Crime Branch, claimed that these IM men were the missing link in the 2006 train blasts investigation. According to Maria, interrogations had revealed that the IM was a SIMI offshoot and that they were receiving assistance from across the border. Maria elaborated the Crime Branch's stand, 'The mention of Pakistani nationals in the 7/11 blasts charge sheet are actually these people. They had told their associates, who were later arrested, that they were Pakistanis.'

A picture taken during the press conference at the Azad Maidan Police Club showed Mumbai Police Commissioner Hasan Gafoor shaking hands with Senior Police Inspector Arun Chavan, congratulating the Mumbai Crime Branch for this important IM breakthrough. At the extreme left is a gleeful Maria.

When the Crime Branch cracked down on the IM module, not a single drop of blood had been spilt. The IM was responsible for most blasts across the country since the 20 July 2005 train bombings in Jaunpur, Uttar Pradesh. Some of the IM-engineered blasts included the ones in Bangalore, Jaipur, Ahmedabad, Surat and Delhi, which killed hundreds of people. The Crime Branch operation had lasted two months, and assisted by the Delhi Police, it arrested Afzal Usmani, aged thirty-two, Sadiq Israr

Shaikh, aged thirty-one, Arif Badar, aged thirty-eight, Zakir Sheikh, aged twenty-eight, and Ansar Badshah, aged thirty-one.

The breakthrough for the police were the stolen cars found in Navi Mumbai that had been used in the Ahmedabad blasts in Gujarat. The police then tried tracing local car thieves, which led them to the IM members. The police had by then recovered about 10 kilograms of gelatin and ammonium nitrate, fifteen detonators, 8 kilograms of ball bearings, four fully activated electronic circuits, one sub-machine carbine, two .38 revolvers and thirty-eight cartridges, from a paan shop in Kurla.

These men were charged under sections of the Indian Explosives Act, MCOCA and the Indian Penal Code. Seven of them, including Riyaz Bhatkal, Amir Raza, Iqbal Bhatkal, Shahrukh, Khalid, Shahzad and Ariz Khan, were also named as accused, but the police had been unable to locate them. As the commissioner of police, Hasan Gafoor, said, 'They were definitely up to something.'

Deputy Chief Minister and state Home Minister R.R. Patil announced a reward of Rs 5 lakh for the investigating team. The Bharatiya Janta Party general secretary Gopinath Munde, demanded a CBI probe into the entire issue so that 'the truth is revealed.'

~

In the months that followed, it became evident that the two groups—the thirteen accused arrested and the twenty-three IM members—had nothing to do with one another. Members of the IM denied knowing Faisal and the other accused by the ATS of planting the bombs.

Meanwhile, the rift between the Crime Branch and the ATS had widened; the ATS refused to acknowledge the role of the IM in the blasts, at least in public circles. If Sadiq was actually a former SIMI member living in Govandi, where the bombs had been assembled in the house of another former SIMI member, Mohammed Ali, how was it that not a single one of the thirteen men accused by the ATS knew him?

But Sadiq's video caught the ATS on the wrong foot. Though the ATS knew that Sadiq had told the Crime Branch that the IM had played a role in the blasts, he had not given precise details publicly. Five months after his arrest, the ATS finally took Sadiq into custody, on 21 February 2009, to investigate his role in the blasts. The video's release on 27 February, just a week later, inside an interrogation room, was timely. The exclusive video kept replaying for days. It seemed that it was done to pressurize the ATS on television.

Thakare had made up his mind. He sprung into action and filed an application in court asking for the media to be barred from reporting anything till the time they completed Sadiq's interrogation. On the next date, when Sadiq was produced in court, he claimed innocence after which his statement was recorded.

Three months later, the ATS filed a report before the MCOCA court saying that Sadiq had no role in the blasts and should be discharged from the case. The report said an independent investigation by the agency had been unable to corroborate Sadiq's claims.

First of all, none of the thirteen accused had mentioned Sadiq's role in the blasts. Second, the ATS said that Sadiq's confession mentioned using 5-litre pressure cookers for the blasts, which were purchased for Rs 300 from a particular shop. But when the ATS officials went to the location, the shop owners and salesmen told them that no 5-litre cooker— branded or local—was priced at Rs 300 when Sadiq claimed to have purchased them. The ATS said that the shop from which Sadiq claimed to have bought the bags for the bombs was in fact a shoe shop.

With regard to the making of the bombs, Sadiq's confession mentioned a flat in Sewree, rented by Abu Rashid. The ATS, however, said that when they went there, they found that a man named Iklak Shaikh and his son, Abu Rashid, lived in the flat with their families. It also said that the timer device mentioned by Sadiq used in the blasts was different from the timer device found in the ATS's investigation. The MCOCA court accepted the ATS's assertions and discharged Sadiq from the 7/11 blasts case on 11 May 2009.

However, a study of the confession statements reveals that SIMI members Ehtesham Siddiqui, one of the alleged bomb planters, and Mohammed Ali, in whose house the bombs were allegedly assembled, had both claimed to know IM co-founder, Riyaz Bhatkal. Ehtesham had allegedly said that he had met Riyaz regarding the training camps he wanted to set up and Mohammed Ali claimed to have met him when in need of money. So, were the 7/11 blasts orchestrated by Riyaz Bhatkal and his men from the IM or was it the former SIMI men already facing trial for the blasts, or was there an unestablished link between the two?

Riyaz was also named in a dossier handed over at a meeting between the then foreign secretaries of India and Pakistan, Nirupama Rao and Salman Bashir, in February 2010. The document, called 'Dossiers of terrorists based in Pakistan and involved in terror cases in India', stated that Riyaz Bhatkal arranged for the delivery of 35 kilograms of RDX used in the 7/11 blasts. It also mentioned that the emails sent by the IM to various media houses, just before the IM carried out blasts in other cities, were all sent on Riyaz's instructions.

Four years after Sadiq's deposition in court, in August 2013, another IM member Yasin Bhatkal was arrested for his role in Mumbai's triple blasts case in July 2011 and Pune's German Bakery blast case. Yasin too claimed that the Riyaz Bhatkal–led IM was responsible for the 7/11 blasts. He said that the Azamgarh unit of the IM, led by Sadiq Israr Shaikh and Atif Amin, who was killed in the 2008 Batla House encounter, led the attack. But this time no one investigated his claims. The ATS considered the thirteen people they had arrested guilty of the 7/11 blasts, and nothing could shake their belief.

16

Death of an Iconoclast

A flatbed truck was decorated with thousands of flowers. Men in crisp khaki uniforms walked alongside the vehicle through the by-lanes of Dadar, the Marathi heartland in central Mumbai. It was the funeral procession of the fifty-four-year-old martyr, Hemant Karkare, chief of the ATS. Karkare, a gracious, humble and honest officer, had taken bullets to his neck and shoulders as he fought the terrorists who laid siege to Mumbai on 26 November 2008.

His body reached his home in Dadar around 7.30 a.m., where his colleagues waited, red-eyed. At 10.20 a.m., the funeral procession began. The Mumbai police commissioner, Hasan Gafoor, and the director general of police, A.N. Roy, carried the casket to Shivaji Park, through a crowd of people who were chanting slogans and weeping silently.

The chief minister of Maharashtra, Vilasrao Deshmukh, the deputy chief minister, R.R. Patil, and several other politicians and senior IPS officers were also present at the funeral. Protocol was observed, with salutations and the band performing, while people paid their last respects to Karkare.

All those who had worked with him were there for one last glimpse of the man who had treated them with so much respect.

Everyone broke down, except his wife, Kavita Karkare. Her calm and composed face concealed the storm raging inside her. She wanted to scream and cry loudly, but chose not to. She stood silently as Aakash, their son, carried out the last rites. Her husband was a martyr and you don't cry for a martyr's death, she thought. Instead, she stared at her husband's corpse until the fire engulfed his body.

Two more pyres were lit in different parts of the state that day. Both were police officers killed in the gruesome terror strike: Inspector Vijay Salaskar of the Mumbai Crime Branch and Additional Commissioner of Police Ashok Kamte. The encounter between Karkare, his men and one of the terrorists was narrated later by Constable Arun Jadhav, the lone survivor of the ambush.

On that fateful night of 26/11, Jadhav accompanied Karkare, Kamte and Salaskar in a jeep that was attacked by two terrorists near the Cama and Albless Hospital at CST. Karkare was at home having dinner when he got the call. He had reached late after finishing his meeting at Malabar Hill with R.R. Patil. Just then, he received a message about gun firing near the Taj Mahal Palace hotel in Colaba, a popular tourist hang out in south Mumbai. He promptly left the dining table, his food half eaten, and rushed to the spot. On reaching Colaba, he was told about another round of firing near CST. He ordered his driver to turn around towards CST. There, a police constable briefed him that the terrorists were on a foot overbridge connecting a by-lane adjacent to the heritage Times of India building and CST railway station. Karkare immediately got in touch with the deputy commissioner of railway police,

Vasant Koregaonkar, and asked him to rush to the station and take charge. By this time, it had sunk in that it was not a case of ordinary gun firing, but a massive terror attack on the city and the terrorists were spread over different locations. Meanwhile, Deputy Commissioner of Police (DCP) Sanjay Mohite reached the spot along with Salaskar on hearing about the firing and hand grenade explosions. Mohite rushed towards Cama Hospital where he met Kamte, Karkare and Salaskar. The three police officers moved towards the Special Branch office, behind St Xavier's College, while Mohite and a few others were ordered to stay put. They stopped a blue-coloured police Toyota Qualis and proceeded further. Salaskar drove the vehicle, while Kamte sat on the front seat next to him. Karkare sat in the back seat and Jadhav sat in the rear of the vehicle. Three more people—a sub-inspector, a constable and a driver—were also present in the vehicle.

As the police proceeded in the Qualis, a message on the wireless stated that a red Maruti Swift car was parked outside the police headquarters and could potentially have a bomb in it. As they drove towards St Xavier's College, via the Special Branch office, two terrorists hiding in the bushes suddenly opened fire at the vehicle. Since everything had happened in a fraction of a second and they didn't have the time to fight back, the three officers were left grievously injured. The terrorists immediately opened the doors of the vehicle and pulled the injured officers out on to the road. They hijacked the vehicle and fired another round at the police. The ATS chief, despite having put on a bulletproof vest, sustained fatal injuries.

The scale and audacity of the 26/11 terror strike stunned the world. For the first time, a city was attacked using assault rifles, including AK-47s and hand grenades, in several places at the same time. The locations were high-profile targets—the extremely busy CST, the landmark Taj Mahal Palace hotel at the Gateway of India, Leopold Cafe, the luxurious Oberoi Trident at Nariman Point and the Chabad House of the Jews. One hundred and sixty-six people were killed and 500 others were injured in the well-co-coordinated attacks by the LeT. The attacks were aimed at getting international attention as the terrorists had targeted foreign nationals.

Karkare's death was a big setback to ongoing investigations into the Malegaon blasts of 2008. Karkare had broken the tradition of arresting only Muslims for terror cases and had pitched a bold theory about the existence of saffron terror groups. Dismissing the investigations of his predecessors into terror cases, Karkare had dared to arrest Sadhvi Pragya Singh Thakur and Lieutenant Colonel Shrikant Purohit for their alleged involvement in the 2008 Malegaon blasts—a deed that upset many politicians, and came much before Aseemanand's confession. The Bharatiya Janata Party labelled him a *gaddar* (traitor), and claimed that he was blaming Hindus at the behest of some Muslim politicians who wanted attention and votes in the upcoming Lok Sabha elections.

A few days before his death, Karkare was defending the allegations of torture by the ATS, made by Sadhvi Pragya Singh Thakur, in the special court hearing the Malegaon 2008 case. He was under immense pressure to not pursue the Hindu terror angle, but Karkare stayed firm. Just a day before his death, he had met the national security adviser, M.K. Narayanan, and the chief of army intelligence in New Delhi to discuss the investigations and the findings in this case.

Many questioned his work in the 2008 Malegaon blasts case. Sadly, a victim of Islamic terror, he did not live to defend his investigation.

17

Death of Hope

The courtroom was packed with people who had come to witness the 26/11 trial. Relatives of two of the accused stood in the corner of the courtroom, anxious about the fate of their loved ones. Shahid Azmi, the lawyer representing Fahim Ansari and Sabahuddin Shaikh, accused of providing logistical support to the ten terrorists who entered India from Pakistan to carry out the attacks, stood in the same corner. Shahid was discussing some details of the case with the accused and trying to assure them that there was hope.

Shahid had become both popular and notorious in the police and legal world, by taking up the cases of young men accused of being involved in terror activities. Even though he had only been practising law for the last seven years, he had already secured acquittal his clients in more than fourteen terror cases. He had built a reputation for taking on the fights of young Muslims implicated in terror cases.

The prosecution had put forward the theory that Ansari had made maps of the city and handed them to Shaikh in Nepal, in January 2008, ten months before the terror attacks. Shaikh had then handed over the same maps to the key conspirator of the attacks, Zaki-ur-Rehman Lakhvi, in Pakistan. According to them, the maps were subsequently passed on to the terrorists who carried out the attacks in Mumbai. They claimed to have recovered one of the maps from Abu Ismail's pocket. By now, Special Public Prosecutor Ujjwal Nikam had already examined a witness, Nooruddin Shaikh, who claimed to have met Ansari in Nepal and had seen him hand over the maps to Shaikh.

Now it was Shahid's turn to cross-examine the witness. He got up from his seat, looking ruthless. He was known for taking cases apart through his cross-examinations. 'Do you have any tangible proof of his visit to Nepal?' he demanded. Nooruddin had no answer.

Shahid then turned to the prosecution. 'Why did the map, recovered from the right-hand side pocket of slain terrorist Abu Ismail's trouser bear no bloodstains, creases or folds?' he asked. 'His clothes were completely bloodied, especially waist down,' he pointed out. 'How could the police recover the map, spotless, with no creases on it?'

The staff in the courtroom grimaced and the judge pleaded with him to wear gloves as Shahid picked up Ismail's bloodied clothes and underwear with his bare hands and held them up for the entire court to see. There was no way the map could have been recovered from the garments unstained—the map had been prepared and planted by the police. Shahid had made his point.

This argument was the final nail in the coffin and paved the way for the release of both the accused.

At this juncture, someone else was paying careful attention to Shahid's performance in the courtroom. He noted how successfully Shahid was picking at loopholes in cases that portrayed Muslims as terrorists. Shahid was a threat and needed to be eliminated permanently.

~

Far away in Malaysia, a phone rang. After three rings, a man picked up the phone and listened carefully to the person on the other side. After a few seconds, he put the phone down and crossed the room to his computer. He opened his email and downloaded an attachment. It was the picture of a lawyer, Shahid Azmi, posing in his courtroom attire. Santosh Shetty, a former Chhota Rajan aide, had just been given his next job.

One of the first things Shetty did after receiving his assignment was to contact his trusted associate, Bharat Nepali, an up-and-coming assassin. Nepali called himself a 'patriot don'; he gladly accepted the job and informed his sharpshooters in Mumbai. The picture was passed on to Hasmukh Solanki alias Rohit. Rohit called up two more people, Devendra Jagtap alias JD and Pintu Dagle.

~

It was 11 February 2010 and Shahid was looking forward to a three-day vacation. He told reporters in court that day to meet him after three days, as he was leaving the city. He got into his car and told the driver to take him home. As the car pulled up inside the gate of Taximen's Colony, he got down and waited for the driver to park the car. He then collected the files from the back seat, dropped them on the table in his office, a short walk from his house, and headed home to his mother.

Around 7.30 p.m., a man called up Shahid's office and asked his assistant, who had picked up the phone, about

Shahid's whereabouts. When the man replied that he wasn't in the office, the caller insisted on getting Shahid's residential address as he wanted to discuss a case with the thirty-two-year-old lawyer.

Shahid entered the living room in his house and sat on the couch. 'Freshen up,' his mother told him. 'Let me get some snacks for you.' Shahid was very fond of his one-year-old niece and would play with her after returning from work. But today he had no time. As soon as he sat down to eat, the doorbell rang. His peon, Inder, informed him that three people were waiting for him at his office. The men had told him they were in a hurry and had an important case to discuss with him. Shahid was usually visited by troubled or distressed people who needed legal advice urgently. He would try to assuage their worries and make it a point to meet them as soon as possible. Today was no exception. Shahid left his food untouched, and without changing out of his courtroom attire, he hurried towards the office in building number 2. The peon had already asked the three men to wait outside Shahid's cabin. The men had retreated to a secluded corner of the office as they waited for him to arrive.

As soon as he had sat down in his office, he asked Inder to send the men into his cabin. Two men entered, while one waited outside. Shahid asked both men to sit down and invited the third man to come inside too. He refused. When Shahid asked the men about the case they had come to discuss, they pulled out their revolvers and pumped five rounds of bullets into his body. All the three men ran out of the office. Horrified, Inder and the watchman ran towards the shooters, but the men raised their guns and threatened to shoot them too. They fled the scene and jumped into a waiting autorickshaw.

Inder then ran towards Shahid's home, crying and shouting for help. 'Bhai ko goli maar di, bhai ko goli maar di

(Bhai has been shot),' he cried. Hearing the cries, Shahid's mother rushed outside. As Inder told her about the attack, she ran towards the office, only to see her son lying on his chair, soaked in his own blood. 'Allah, *mere bacche ko bachao, mere bacche ko bachao* (God, save my child),' she screamed, over and over again. Within minutes, Shahid's assistant, Shareef, arrived at the office and helped her carry an injured Shahid to his car. They took him to Rajawadi Hospital in Ghatkopar. But it was too late. Shahid was declared dead on arrival.

Breaking news flashed on the television channels: the lawyer representing some of the 26/11 case accused had been murdered. Hundreds of frantic phone calls were exchanged between the families of the men Shahid was defending. '*Ab hamara kya hoga? Ab hamare liye kaun ladega?* (What will happen to us? Who will fight for us?)' they fretted.

Shahid's murder stunned the legal fraternity as well. Everyone demanded to know why the police had not taken any steps to protect him after all the threatening calls he had complained about. Gangster Ravi Pujari had even sent men to his home to intimidate him. It seemed that Shahid's death served both the state and the gangsters' purpose. He, who had laid bare the brutality of the state, exposed their incompetence in building watertight cases, was now gone forever. It was soon discovered that Shahid had tried to contact the police commissioner, A.N. Roy, to report these threats, but he was not granted a meeting.

The only way to silence the critics, social activists and Shahid's supporters was to apprehend the shooters. The Mumbai Crime Branch completed its investigation within a month and declared that JD, Pintu Dagle and Hasmukh Solanki had killed Shahid. Vinod Vichare had conducted the reconnaissance before the killing. On 9 March, the Crime

Branch arrested Solanki, allegedly a close aide of gangster Bharat Nepali.

Solanki was promised Rs 1 lakh for the killing and had planned the shooting for one and a half months. The team first met at the Devidayal Garden in Mulund (west). Vichare was given the job of receiving the contract money and of keeping an eye on Shahid's movements. Hanging around the Sessions Court and Shahid's office in Kurla, Vichare spent several days studying his movements. Two days before the killing, Shetty gave JD the green signal to go ahead with the plan.

The Crime Branch said that Solanki went to a cyber cafe in Mulund (west) and accessed an email account with two images of Shahid on the eve of the murder. Solanki saved the pictures on his pen drive and shared them with JD and Dagle. Dagle and Vichare had no previous criminal record and had been roped in to avoid suspicion. Vichare, Solanki's childhood friend and neighbour in Mulund, was seen spying on Shahid by a resident of the colony, who came forward only after Vichare was arrested.

The Mumbai Crime Branch said that Bharat Nepali agreed to kill Shahid as he was trying to establish himself in the crime world with a high-profile murder. He had broken away from Rajan only a few months ago and this murder was the breakthrough he desperately needed. After Nepali split from his boss in December 2009, he had taken along with him two of Rajan's most influential and widely networked aides— Santosh Shetty and Vijay Shetty.

Chhota Rajan was known to have previously executed similar killings of Muslims, who either owed allegiance to Dawood Ibrahim or were involved in terror cases, to project himself as a patriot. And Shahid had fought several cases on behalf of Muslims, including high-profile cases like the

2002 Ghatkopar blast case, the 2003 Mulund train blast, the 7/11 train blasts, the 2006 Malegaon blasts, the Aurangabad arms haul and the 26/11 attacks.

After Shahid Azmi's death, the 7/11 trial resumed and, from the prosecution's point of view, went on more smoothly than before. Shahid, who was representing six of the accused in the train blasts case, had raised questions about several claims by the ATS at the outset. He had branded ATS witnesses as fake and planted, noting that a main witness had also deposed in three other blast cases. 'How is it possible that this man is always at the right place at the right time?' Shahid had articulated during one of his interviews.

Shahid had come under the scanner of intelligence agencies after taking up the 7/11 and Malegaon blasts cases. Given his background, he was suspected of receiving ISI funds. However, they failed to gather any evidence to support this claim.

The Shetty duo, responsible for Shahid's death, was now operating out of Singapore and Bangkok, with a finger in the narcotics trade in South Asia, and they were raking in money. In the past few months, some of the key men who worked for Rajan had switched camps—Nepali's pay was better. What also worked in Nepali's favour were a few sensational shoot-outs he had carried out, shortly after the split. In the first week of February, Nepali had Jamim Shah, a television entrepreneur in Nepal and a close Dawood aide, killed. There were rumours that Nepali had been helped by Indian intelligence agencies in this operation. Shahid Azmi's murder was just another way for Nepali to establish himself as a 'patriotic don'.

Santosh Shetty was deported for Shahid's murder from Bangkok in April 2011 and was imprisoned in Arthur Road Jail, which also housed the accused in the 7/11 case. The friction between the accused and Shetty was palpable. They considered beating him up, but restrained themselves as it would invite trouble from prison authorities. But they constantly cold-shouldered him. So when Shetty organized a birthday treat and ordered biryani for everyone in prison, the thirteen men refused to eat the food. For jail inmates, good food is a luxury and their refusal shocked everyone, including jail officials. The 7/11 accused had been deeply hurt and affected by Shahid's death.

No one has still been convicted of the murder of Shahid Azmi, as the trial against the accused is yet to begin. Before Nepali could be convicted for the killing, he was murdered by Shetty over a dispute. In 2015, Shetty was discharged by the Bombay High Court in Shahid's murder case. There wasn't enough evidence to conduct a trial against him.

18

A Witness, a Confession and a Pressure Cooker

Prosecution witness no. 74. The plump thirty-year-old man's fair skin flushed in the March heat. He seemed nervous.

'Pay attention, Mr Parmar,' a man, clad in black, sporting the white shirt and band of a lawyer, reprimanded him gently. But Vishal Parmar was too busy staring out of the court's fifth-floor window at Elphinstone College, visible through the trees.

'*Ji?*' Parmar suddenly looked up at him.

'I asked if you know the relationship your boss shared with the police?' Avinash Rasal, one of the three defence lawyers representing Ehtesham, repeated.

'I do not have any knowledge of it,' Parmar said, eager to escape the suffocating stand. To stand in the witness box and face a gruelling cross-examination by the 'other side' was a trying exercise, and had more to do with the witness's stamina and state of mind than the actual testimony itself.

'But you must be aware that he was called as a *panch* witness by the police in this case before. On 2 November 2006.'

The date was as important as the question.

During his examination by the ATS special public prosecutor, Raja Thakare, Parmar had narrated how, on the fateful day of 11 July 2006, two men, one carrying a black Rexine bag, boarded the first-class general compartment of the Virar-bound local from Churchgate station. The train was scheduled to depart from platform no. 3 at 5.19 p.m. He claimed that the men had hurriedly got off the train without the Rexine bag at Dadar station.

The ATS had cited Parmar as an eyewitness in the case. But his statement had come three months after the blasts. By this time, thirteen men had been arrested by the ATS, eleven had allegedly confessed to their role in the bomb blasts, and their confessional statements had been recorded. To justify the delay in coming to the police, Parmar claimed that he read about the black Rexine bags used in the blasts much later and approached the police only after finding out which police station was investigating the case. It was just a coincidence that his immediate boss, moneylender Mukesh Walji Rabadia, was a regular panch witness for the police and had, in fact, witnessed the alleged seizures made from the house where the bombs had allegedly been assembled. Rabadia passed away a few months before he could testify in court. The defence lawyer was alluding to these seizures, but Parmar either didn't know about them or had decided to stick to his story. He did not know whether the police had called his boss before 2 November 2006, he reiterated.

He claimed he remembered the 7/11 incident because one of the two men with the bags had asked him if the local train standing in front of them went to Virar, and then, while boarding the train, the Rexine bag had brushed against his leg.

Sitting in the dock was Ehtesham Siddiqui, identified by Parmar as the one carrying the bag. All the accused men had been provided truncated copies of the charge sheet, with the names and addresses of the witnesses hidden in white ink to protect them. There was little the accused could find out about the witnesses to help their defence.

'Do you remember seeing any person keeping any bag on the rack?' the next lawyer, Abdul Wahab Khan, asked.

'I don't remember,' Parmar answered.

'Would it be correct if I said it is common for someone to make inquiries about the train timings from a fellow passenger, get pushed around during rush hour and carry luggage on a train? Aren't quarrels and abuses common in trains?'

'Yes, it would be correct.'

Khan grinned, revealing his teeth, and sat down.

Prakash Shetty questioned Parmar next. Shetty, the lawyer defending six of the thirteen accused, had been the only constant in the case for the defence. The rest, including Khan and advocate Sharif Shaikh, became part of the trial after the death of Shahid. The white tika on the forehead of the short, dark, pot-bellied, bearded advocate had never come between him and his clients. He was a man of few words and had seen very few failures in his four-decade career. Shetty rarely represented the small fry; underworld cases, like those involving Dawood Ibrahim, were his forte. That the Jamiat's legal aid cell had managed to get him on board for this trial was an achievement in itself.

'So, Mr Parmar,' Shetty looked up from the papers in front of him, his rimless spectacles touching the ridge of his nose. 'When did you hear about the blasts?'

'The same day, [at] night, around 9–9.15 p.m.,' Parmar replied.

'Didn't you realize that one of the bombs had gone off in the same Virar fast you were travelling in, just ahead of Mira Road?' Shetty asked.

'I don't remember.'

Shetty was pointing out the extraordinary coincidence of the situation—barring one, all other witnesses, including the taxi drivers who had allegedly ferried the bomb planters from Carter Road to Churchgate, and commuters who had seen the bombs being planted, had recorded their statements more than three months after the blasts. Still, the details they gave were incredibly precise.

'You claimed that it was much later that you came to know about the bags being used in the blasts . . . Do you remember through which paper or channel you first stumbled across this detail?' Shetty pushed on relentlessly.

'No, I don't,' came the reply.

Since they believed that Parmar was lying, the defence also raised several questions about his presence at Churchgate station. In his statement to the police, Parmar had mentioned that he had gone to meet Babban Rankhambe, a compounder at an ENT hospital, with regard to the repayment of a loan given by Parmar's employer. RTI applications filed by Ehtesham later revealed that no Babban Rankhambe worked at the hospital.

More than two years after the above exchange, Raja Thakare handed over a document to the judge. It was an exchange of letters between the ATS officers and the chief medical officer of the ENT Hospital. The letters showed that a Baban Rongya

'Kamble' worked as a laboratory assistant at the hospital. Parmar had also recently changed his statement to say that he had gone to meet this Baban Kamble, not Rankhambe, at the hospital, on the day of the blasts. Another RTI application filed by Ehtesham revealed that Kamble did indeed work at the hospital, but had not come to work on the day of the blasts. Ehtesham's RTI inquiries were testing the prosecution's patience.

'How does it matter if he was present that day for duty or not?' Thakare later argued. 'What matters [is that] he was a BMC [Brihanmumbai Municipal Corporation] employee and in a position to take a loan from Parmar's employer; the applications are inconsequential.'

But more information from RTI applications questioned Parmar's testimony. He had been a panch witness in at least four previous cases, starting with a 2006 case at the Mahalaxmi police station. As for his employer, Rabadia, most of the cases he testified in involved Police Inspector Vasant Tajne, also one of the investigators in the 7/11 case.

Thakare continued to defend his witness. 'Even if it is established that his boss had been a regular panch for the investigating agency and he had tried to claim ignorance, does that stop [Parmar] from travelling in the suburban railways and discredit his testimony?'

Under Indian law, the statement of a person under oath is credible only if it withstands the scrutiny of cross-examination. Shetty and Khan feared that the eyewitnesses had been tutored and were not credible. They quizzed several witnesses during the course of the trial and were successful in questioning the prosecution's theory on several vital aspects.

Still, they did not succeed. Judge Y.D. Shinde, in his judgement four years later, would observe that the lack of corroboration from the hospital must have been a result of the phonetic difference in the name. The witness must have said Baban Rongya Kamble, but everyone in court, including the judge, thought he was saying Babban Rankhambe. Parmar was a truthful witness and his employer's relationship with the police would not discredit his testimony, unless a specific motive was proved.

~

Despite citing over 2000 witnesses in the charge sheet, Thakare closed his case in the spring of April 2012 after examining only 192 of them, sparing everyone the May heat. Thakare had done the best he could with the evidence provided to him by the ATS. The 7/11 trial was by far the most voluminous case he had ever handled and he believed that 192 witnesses were enough to prove the mountain of allegations against the thirteen men.

These 192 people included railway officials, who ascertained that the suburban railway line had lost Rs 85,61,039 because of the blasts, officials and injured travellers who had watched the carnage as it unfolded, eyewitnesses to the preparation and planting of the bombs and a witness to the meetings in which over thirteen men conspired against the city. The number of injured was so high that their experiences were recorded in 258 affidavits to save time. There were doctors who had operated on countless injured persons after the blasts, and doctors who had treated the accused during the years they spent in custody. Panch witnesses testified to the seizure of certain articles from the blast sites, the bodies of the dead, the injured and the homes of the accused. Experts from the Forensic Science Laboratory who had deconstructed the explosives from the blast site, men connected to the hawala money trail from Pakistan and Saudi Arabia, the DCPs who had recorded the confessions of eleven of the thirteen accused, and finally, Thakare's star witnesses: the investigating officers he trusted would tie up all the loose ends of the case by justifying limitations while investigating the case.

Confessions

'Concocted. False. Made-up and improbable.' For eight years, these words were bounced around the courtroom against Raja Thakare's witnesses. In a case where the prosecution was leaning heavily on confessional statements to corroborate the series of events, the statements had to be watertight. For a confession to be accepted by a court of law, it should not only be true, but should also be voluntary. Unfortunately for Thakare, the eleven men who had allegedly confessed had disassociated themselves from these 'confessions' the moment they had signed them.

'Not a single investigator said that any of them had any desire to make a confession,' Shetty pointed out in court. 'Now, after more than seventy days of being in custody, within days of the MCOCA being applied, under which confessions are permissible, they start singing like parrots?'

All eleven of the accused decided to confess to the ATS in October 2006. Statements of the ATS's most important witnesses were recorded the very next month.

The defence had several arguments questioning the veracity of the confessions. All thirteen of the accused were Urdu-speaking Muslims, hailing from a similar socio-economic background. Yet, all the 'confessions' were in Hindi, interspersed with Marathi and Sanskrit words. They cited certain examples: words like *pitaji*, *vyakti*, *vivah* and *atyachar* that appeared in the confessions instead of the Urdu words *walid*, *admi*, *shaadi* and *zulm*, raising more doubts about the authenticity of the confessions. Further, in each piece of correspondence before, during or after the recording of the confessions, the order of the sections applied was the same. All letters issued by the police had the same additions and retractions. The questions asked to the eleven accused during their interrogations were similar, and the 'confessions' were all written in the same format, despite the fact that they were recorded by seven different officers. How was it possible that seven people made the same exact mistakes and corrections in all eleven statements?

Advocate Khan made this observation in court—that all the police officers who recorded the confessions of the accused made the same errors in the format of the memos. 'I wonder how seven officers were all thinking on similar lines,' he said wryly.

Just because a few things were common did not mean the entire 'essence' of the document was false, the prosecution argued. 'If the confessions were actually concocted, these dissimilarities and discrepancies would not exist to begin with,' Thakare responded angrily. 'Why only eleven confessions when we would have gotten all thirteen? Why would there be a single mistake? Why would we even attempt to get the history and geography of the accused?'

Judge Shinde ruled that the language of the confessions was not a point of contention. He said that only four of the accused were unfamiliar with Marathi, as they were not from Mumbai, and all of them could have chosen words different from the ones they used regularly so that the officer could understand. He reiterated the point of the prosecution—the essence of the statements could not be ignored.

Yug Mohit Chaudhry, an articulate and astute human rights lawyer with a PhD on the Irish poet W.B. Yeats, called in as a defence counsel in this case, silently fumed. 'Without these confessions,' he remarked, 'I'd complete my arguments in a day.' While Chaudhry did not conduct the trial in the case, he was asked to step in during the final stage of arguments.

The Pressure Cooker and Triggering Device

On 30 September, the ATS had announced in its press conference that pressure cooker bombs were used in the blasts. They had even emphasized the name of the brand— Kanchan. But these pressure cookers did not feature in a single document in the court records—not one confession or document mentioned the words 'pressure cooker'. Instead, the lethal mixture was put in 'household utensils', the ATS claimed in the charge sheet, two months after the press conference. A pressure cooker was seized from Mohammed Ali's Govandi home, where the bombs were allegedly made.

Yet, eight years later, during the final arguments, Thakare affirmed that pressure cookers were probable utensils in which the bombs could have been stored. He called an expert to the stand to show how a bomb could be made using explosives, detonators, a power source and proper triggering mechanisms, if a pressure cooker was used as the container.

Another contentious point in the prosecution's case was the ambiguity about the triggering device used—it was unclear whether a timer set off the bomb or a remote control. The judge ruled that it would have been impossible for the ATS to be certain about the container and triggering device in light of the intensity of the explosions. Ironically, one of the reasons cited to discharge the IM man, Sadiq Israr Shaikh, was the difference in the triggering device stated by him and the one used in the blasts.

Pacing around the special court, Chaudhry asked, 'The police had access to the accused for months ... If these were the real perpetrators, wouldn't they spill the beans on such basic details, such as the shop where they bought the Rexine bags from or what kind of containers were used to make the bombs?'

Thakare answered the question: the details were not in their confessional statements simply because the accused did not give any specifications. Judge Shinde accepted Thakare's contention, adding that the absence of these details only increased the authenticity of the confessions.

To Iran and Back

A visit to Iran in 2005, undertaken by four of the thirteen accused, turned out to be an indefensible piece of evidence against them. The accused claimed that the voyage was a pilgrimage; the prosecution insisted that the trip was merely a camouflage for other goals.

Investigators discovered that Shia Muslims, who revered Imam Reza, visited Iran for Ziyarat (pilgrimage). The four accused were Sunni Muslims, not Shia. Further, all four accused had used the same group of tour operators and agents to visit Iran, though at different points in time. All four travelled individually, not in groups, as is common during pilgrimages. The prosecution called the tour operators and agents to court. They used that testimony to assert that the Iran trip was not a pilgrimage, but a ruse to sneak into Pakistan from Iran.

The defence team pointed out that the witnesses were incorrect—it was not true that Sunnis never went for the

Ziyarat and that a pilgrim would compulsorily go for *Niyaz* (food at a place of religious significance). 'One could go for another meal in the morning or evening and, therefore, not have the stamp of Niyaz,' they reasoned. They told the court that the absence of the Niyaz stamp was not conclusive proof that a person had not gone to Iran for pilgrimage, but to Pakistan for training in a terrorist camp. Ultimately, the judge overruled the defence. Ordinarily, a person visiting the tomb of Imam Reza at Mashhad in Iran would partake of the Niyaz, and obtain the important stamp, the court ruled. It was a symbol of pride, something to show to others, the judge added.

The judge went on to draw parallels in the Indian context, explaining that tourists visiting historical monuments, like the Taj Mahal and the Red Fort, or religious sites would definitely take photos of themselves with these monuments in the background. If the accused had gone on the pilgrimage, they would have the stamp, the judge concluded. He also saw no reason why the witnesses, all Muslims with no previous contact with the police, would wish to falsely implicate the accused.

Deconstructing a Case via Right to Information

If there was ever a case that used the 2005 RTI Act to counter every single accusation of the prosecution, it was the 7/11 Mumbai train blasts case. The defence of these thirteen men hinged on the RTI applications they had filed from jail.

Over their longer-than-eight-year incarceration, the accused filed 1785 applications, with over 500 directly related to the case.

The applications were used to counter eyewitness claims, to check the authenticity of their confessions and, among other things, to reveal probable 'corruption' among crucial officers in the case. However, the fact that the ATS did not come under the RTI Act's purview, proved to be a huge hurdle for the accused. Many applications had to be filed indirectly to shed light on the workings of other government departments, which weren't exempt from the scrutiny of the Act—such as local police stations, railway stations and government hospitals. Among the many startling revelations that the applications threw up was the fact that several crucial witnesses, including several eyewitnesses, had a criminal record.

The whereabouts of several officers could not be directly ascertained, so RTI applications were filed to get the logbooks for their vehicles, which catalogued their precise movements. For example, Tanveer obtained logs to show how one officer had actually been on bandobast duty despite claiming that he was recording Tanveer's confession during that time. An RTI application's reply was used to show that medical check-ups were not done before the confessions, which left open the possibility that the accused had been tortured before the confessions, rendering the confessions involuntary. In 2008, the accused claimed to have been beaten up during their transfer from Arthur Road Jail to other prisons across Maharashtra. The evidence of this attack was revealed through an RTI application, which listed the injuries they had sustained during the incident. The details came from the medical examination the accused underwent fifteen–twenty days after the incident.

As more details were revealed through RTI applications, the investigators who testified before the court were questioned again. Police Inspector Arun Khanvilkar had visited the Mahim and Bandra blast sites on the day of the strike and made several inquiries. However, Khanvilkar himself was accused of demanding money from a gangster, Manoj Shivyagnya Prasad Singh, allegedly involved in the narcotics business. He was suspended on 18 February 2010 and reinstated six months later. At the time of his deposition, the order to prosecute him had still not been granted.

Similarly, a departmental inquiry was ongoing against Assistant Police Inspector Nivrutti Kolhatkar and other officers for allegedly attending a party in which well-known gangsters D.K. Rao and Farid Tanasha had been present. Kolhatkar was under suspension during this time. In another case, Vasant Tajne, the ATS police inspector who arrested Kamal, had been suspended from 21 March 1989 to 3 March 1990, when he was with the Crime Branch. According to Tajne, the suspension was the result of a false corruption complaint filed against him and he had been acquitted after a departmental inquiry.

While the RTI applications were extremely helpful for the defence, much of the information procured under the Act turned out to be useless. This included all the information about the movement of police vehicles while investigating the case. The judge observed if a person, i.e. government official, is giving the information, such information is given for the knowledge of the party seeking that information. 'Such information, to my mind, cannot be a substitute for evidence and cannot be considered as evidence proved under the law,' the judge declared. 'If such information is required to be used as evidence of a particular fact, it has to be proved as per the provisions of the Indian Evidence Act.'

The Invisible Pakistanis

Like the 1993 serial blasts and the 26/11 terror attacks, the prosecution and the ministry of external affairs raised the issue of Pakistan's involvement in the 7/11 blasts as well. But there was no solid proof in the form of independent documents like passports of the Pakistanis seized, etc., to show their existence. The Pakistanis were only mentioned in confessions of the accused and witness statements.

The ATS claimed that a Pakistani accused, who they called Salim, had been killed in the Matunga blast. However, there were several families claiming his body. A letter attached to the charge sheet showed that the authorities had sent the remains for digital reconstruction in order to identify the 'correct claimant'. Once Salim's face had been reconstructed, a correction was made to the post-mortem report. He had previously been termed 'Hindu' and 'Unknown'. Now he was Muslim and Salim, and was later buried.

Another Pakistani related to the case, Riyaz Nawabuddin, had been arrested under the Arms Act around the same time as the serial blasts. He revealed to the police that one more Pakistani, Abu Umed, was hiding in Antop Hill, which led to the encounter there. Nawabuddin was deported to Pakistan as soon as he finished serving his sentence in the Arms Act case.

Advocate Khan, who represented Nawabuddin in that case, brought up a damning allegation against the investigating officer, Vasant Tajne. Khan said that Tajne had kicked Nawabuddin in such a way during his interrogation that the man's testicles were shoved into his scrotum. Nawabuddin was sent to judicial custody and then admitted to J.J. Hospital only on 7 October 2006. By this time, gangrene had set in and his testicles had to be removed. Khan further alleged that Tajne had cut a deal with Nawabuddin that if he did not complain about the beating, they would not implicate him in the 7/11 case. The chief investigating officer, Sadashiv Patil, denied any knowledge of Nawabuddin's operation at J.J. Hospital and any forced deals between the investigating officer and the accused.

The ATS relied on the oral testimony of Mohammad Alam Qureshi, Faisal's and Naved's best friend, and Majid's friend Mohammed Shakeel Mehboob to confirm the involvement of Pakistanis in the blasts. While Qureshi had said that he saw a few Pakistanis at Faisal's house, Mehboob said he was there with Majid when they crossed the border with the Pakistanis.

But when Qureshi stood in the witness box, he said that the cops had asked him to identify the photo of a man with a half-burnt face. He was asked to record his statement on 2 November—months after the accused were arrested. Qureshi identified the person as Abu Umed, whom he remembered seeing at Faisal's house. However, the person who died in the blast and the man in the photo was Salim.

The defence also claimed that Qureshi wasn't in town when he was supposed to have witnessed the conspiracy meeting; he had travelled abroad for the first time, to China. One of Khan's sources, from the Worli passport office, had promised details on Qureshi's whereabouts. But the source never got back with the details and cut off all contact with him when Khan insisted. Khan wondered if his phone had been tapped and his source had been dissuaded from helping him.

Each eyewitness was shown two photographs during the investigation: of the body of Abu Umed, killed in the Antop Hill encounter, and the reconstructed image of Salim's face. But none of them, including the train commuters who recorded their statements with the ATS, were able to identify the two men.

Since the 1993 serial blasts case, over thirty accused, including Dawood Ibrahim, Tiger Memon and his wife, Ayub Memon and his wife, have been in hiding in Pakistan. The 26/11 terror case is similar: key players like Hafeez Saeed and Zaki-ur-Rehman Lakhvi, among others, have remained in Pakistan, even though their roles in the terror attack have been clearly identified. Though the police have suggested links to terrorists in Pakistan in the present case, most have only been identified by their first names. The list of Pakistanis supposedly involved in the 7/11 case includes the alleged mastermind Azam Cheema and others like Sohail Shaikh, Aslam, Hafizullah, Sabir, Abu Bakr, Kasam Ali, Ammu Jaan, Ehsanullah, Abu Hasan, Abdul Razzak and Abdul Rehman.

No real progress has been made in ascertaining their location or nabbing them in India or Pakistan. While a lookout circular (used at airports to check if a person travelling is wanted by the police) was issued against all eleven, a red corner notice (an arrest warrant put out by Interpol on behalf of a country) could not be issued due to the lack of precise details, like their addresses, identification marks, etc. The information the ATS had gathered about these suspects was sketchy at best. As a result, the 7/11 case is rarely ever brought up during high-level discussions between India and Pakistan. Only a dossier sent to Pakistan in 2010 showed Riyaz Bhatkal as a wanted accused in the 7/11 train blasts case.

The Almost Perfect Alibi

The defence did not merely deny the charges against the accused, it also tried to establish that the accused were not present in each of the places the ATS claimed they were when the blasts occurred. They even tried deflecting the blame on the IM. But how would they prove this? Who could they bring to the witness box to prove their theory?

The defence team wanted the officer who recorded Sadiq's confessional statement, DCP Vishwas Nangre Patil, to testify in court. But the court ruled that only Sadiq could tell if he was actually behind the blasts. It was evident that Sadiq was unlikely to implicate himself by accepting responsibility for the blasts under oath. But what he did reveal opened up another can of worms.

Sadiq denied every single damning piece of information he had told the Crime Branch and in his televised confession. He stood in the witness box for two days and claimed that he did not know any of the men arrested by the ATS. He had not named them or the Bhatkals in his confession, he said. Khan asked the court to declare him a hostile witness.

During the hearing, Sadiq told the court that the Crime Branch had forced him to speak on video. 'I was given a paper with something written on it and asked to learn it by heart. What was on the paper was linked to the 7/11 blasts. I was given the paper after I was taken to the office of the DCP. Officer Dinesh Kadam of the Crime Branch gave me the story,' Sadiq claimed. 'They asked me to tell this story before a camera . . . they asked me to relax and they shot a video of me telling what was in the paper. It was probably Officer Dhamankar of the Crime Branch, who had burn injuries on his face and hand, who shot the video.'

Sadiq was asked why he was given a fake story by the Crime Branch officers. According to him, officers Dhamankar and Dinesh Kadam, who were part of the ATS earlier, had told him that those arrested in the 7/11 case were falsely accused and that they had not carried out the blasts. Thakare said this was merely hearsay and could not be used as evidence. He accused Sadiq of doing this simply to destroy the case.

By now, three different versions of the events were floating around. In his 2008 interrogation video, leaked on television, Sadiq claimed that the IM 'did it'. Less than a month after the ATS took his custody in the present case, he told Judge Shinde that all the claims made in the video confession were false and that one Atif from Azamgarh had asked him to take responsibility for the blasts to confuse the investigators.

Now, standing in the witness box, on 3 April 2013, Sadiq denied everything, saying that the Crime Branch had forced him to confess to the crime and that the ATS had told him to blame his confession on 'Atif'. Finally, at the end of all the courtroom drama, Judge Shinde noted his observations about Sadiq and the investigation into the IM link. 'It appears that the investigating agency fell prey to the tactics of terrorist organizations to confuse [them] and in their exuberance, another branch of the police may have given an interview in the media. Be that as it may, the fact remains that . . . the investigating machinery in this case, i.e. the ATS, duly took the custody of Sadiq Israr Shaikh in this case and thoroughly questioned him and only when it was established that he had stated falsely about the involvement of the IM, at the behest of one Atif, did they come to the conclusion that he or members of the IM were not responsible for the blasts and therefore they applied for his discharge.'

~

Advocate Khan and the soft-spoken advocate Sharif Shaikh, representing the accused on behalf of Jamiat, almost skipped into court on 26 April 2013. That day, after a long wait, they had with them the all-important break their clients needed—their call data records (CDRs). The records showed that of the five planters, four of them were nowhere near Churchgate railway station on the day of the blasts. It was a perfect alibi for his clients.

In their head, the defence had nailed the case. For the first time in his eighteen-year career, not Khan, but his clients were the brains behind the defence strategy. He had walked his clients' path, done as they suggested and extracted what they wanted from the 192 prosecution witnesses. And he hadn't worked alone. Asif, Ehtesham, Tanveer, Sajid and Abdul Wahid, his clients in prison, spent night after night strategizing and studying papers to discredit the testimony of each and every witness on the stand.

Unlike the others, Faisal, Kamal, Muzzammil and Zameer were not actively involved in their defence. They had left their fate to the extremely experienced and mentally agile Prakash Shetty.

Today, Khan believed they had made two of the most important points in the case—first, by accusing the IM of orchestrating the blasts and then, by revealing the almost-perfect alibi of the accused. 'They weren't on those trains to begin with,' he had tried to show in court. What made this 'win' so much more delectable was how badly the ATS had not wanted them to get the CDRs.

For three months after the accused were arrested, the ATS cited the study of their CDRs as one of the main grounds for keeping them in custody. They had claimed that the accused were in contact with their Pakistani counterparts. Yet, after months of investigation, these records did not figure in the charge sheet.

When the defence filed an application in Judge Shinde's court in 2007, seeking their call data records, the ATS said they would produce only those documents required to prove their case, suggesting that all the records did not support their case. The ATS asserted that the CDRs had nothing to do with the ongoing trial and the defence could not demand documents procured by the ATS. Accepting these arguments, their applications were rejected by the MCOCA court.

The defence subsequently moved the High Court. The ATS's claims before the MCOCA court were dismissed after Advocate General Darius Khambata submitted that the ATS did procure the CDRs, but later destroyed them as they were not relying on them for the case. This had not been mentioned in the MCOCA court. The HC judge galvanized the telecom companies into action, asking them to retrieve the necessary data. Although initially the companies asked the accused to pay an impossible Rs 34 lakh to retrieve the data, the MCOCA court later ordered the companies to provide the data free of cost.

The defence's case was clear—they would use the call records to show the activities of the five bomb planters on the day of the blasts. Faisal, accused of planting the bomb in the 5.36 p.m. Churchgate–Borivali slow train that went off at Jogeshwari, had been in Bandra on 11 July. Asif, accused of planting the bomb in the 5.37 p.m. Virar fast, that exploded at Borivali, was at his workplace, Lokhandwala Construction Company, in Kandivali. Ehtesham, who allegedly planted the bomb in the 5.19 p.m. Virar fast was at his home in Mira Road, only stepping out to go to a cyber cafe after lunch and for his evening prayers at the Shams Masjid—both located in Mira Road. Kamal, charged with planting the bomb in the 5.57 p.m. Virar fast train, which went off near Matunga station, was in his village, Basupatti, through May and June, including the day of the incident.

Naved, who had placed the bomb in the 5.45 p.m. Borivali slow, hadn't requested for his CDRs. Mahanagar Telephone Nigam Limited (MTNL) did not produce Tanveer's CDRs, citing unavailability, although he had requested them.

Once the data was received in April 2013, a whole year after the ATS finished examining their 192 witnesses, the defence leapt into action. Seven representatives of the companies testified with regard to the authenticity of the records.

The eleven accused then, in a rare instance, stepped into the witness boxes to substantiate their alibis. Faisal and Kamal were advised not to act as witnesses by their legal teams.

All the men were hopeful. So far, Judge Y.D. Shinde had allowed all of their requests—a Quran in jail, a *musalla* (rug) on which they could pray, dry fruits during Ramzan and *shirkhurma*, a delicacy made of sweet milk, dry fruits and *seviyan* (vermicelli), for Eid. So what if he asked them to speak from afar, instead of giving them the privilege of coming and making their requests in the witness box? He may have rejected several applications asking for the re-examination of witnesses, but the defence team was hopeful he would now see the case as hollow.

But would Raja Thakare let his case fall apart so easily? His counter to these revelations was simple. 'It is not my case that their mobile phones were with them at the time of doing important operational work. Their confessions specifically state that they were asked not to carry their phones with them. Most of their calls were made from PCOs.'

However, since the men claimed to be carrying their mobiles with them throughout, Thakare said that there was something else being revealed—a connection that defied the defence's claim that there was absolutely no link between the accused. All the men had claimed from the very beginning that they knew nothing about each other. Until this time, the prosecution was relying solely on oral evidence and confessions to establish a connection between the accused. Now, after these call records were revealed, which showed that a few of them made calls to each other, a material link was created between the accused.

So far, Ehtesham had maintained that out of the thirteen accused, he only knew Tanveer as they were both arrested in a SIMI case in 2001. However, later in the trial, he claimed to know Sajid, who had done some 'computer repair work' for him. Sajid was accused of making the circuits for the bombs. The police alleged that the two had exchanged several phone calls around the planning and execution of the train blasts. These calls could now be seen in the records. Thakare said that the theory of the computer repair work was a cover-up for these calls.

During closing arguments, the prosecution came up with yet another theory based on the call records retrieved— that four of the accused were receiving information from 'a command post', set up in a public phone booth near Fauzia Nursing Home in central Mumbai. This data had apparently gone unnoticed by investigators when they scanned through the records during the investigation. The prosecution alleged that Tanveer, who was working at the nursing home until 2000 and lived less than 2 kilometres away in Agripada, was handling the command post. The four who made and received calls from the post were Ehtesham, Sajid, Asif and Zameer.

Citing the CDRs as evidence, the prosecution said that Sajid received calls from the PCO on 6, 10 and 11 July 2006, and that he had made a call to the PCO at 12.20 a.m. on July 12—just hours after the blasts on 11 July. Asif had received calls from this PCO on 10 and 12 July. In addition, the prosecution found it suspicious that Asif's and Ehtesham's mobile SIM cards were not bought in their name.

The defence fended off this allegation by saying that the ATS had set up a special team to study the CDRs immediately after the blasts, but had failed to come up with the 'command post' theory in the last eight years. While Ehtesham had indeed made and received calls to and from the PCO in May, as had Zameer in February, the defence pointed out that these dates were nowhere close to the date of the bombings.

The defence used Tanveer's hospital records to show his location. As per these records, between 1 and 20 July, Tanveer had taken his weekly off on 9 and 16 July, while he was absent on 1, 7, 14 and 18 July. According to the rules of the hospital, if an employee fails to put a thumb impression on the biometric machine while entering the hospital and while leaving, he or she is marked absent. On 9 July, Tanveer had punched in at 11.41a.m, which suggested he had gone to the hospital. Thakare, however, argued that the biometric system was not foolproof. 'A person can mark his attendance and then leave to do something else, and then come back to mark his thumb impression again at the time of leaving. It does not record what he did in between,' he retaliated.

In his final arguments, Thakare questioned the weight of the evidence put forth by the defence.

'The onus is on this court to weigh these two [factors]: on one hand, [we have] evidence in the nature of abstract [factors], like the location of the mobile for which there would not be any means to ascertain who is actually possessing it at the relevant time . . . On the other hand, concrete positive and physical evidence in the nature of deposition of witnesses, whose version can be tested on the touchstone of cross-examination, is before the court,' he summarized.

Judge Shinde listened to these arguments gravely. He placed his hands in front of him and put forth his views in one final observation. He said that Thakare had 'turned the tables' on the accused by completely demolishing the credibility of their alibis, and had instead showed the interconnection between them, exposing the falsity of their defence.

19

Judgement Day

A small nine-year-old girl jumped up and down in the passage connecting the old, three-storey secretariat building to the comparatively new, five-storey structure inside the City Civil and Sessions Court complex. Despite the difference in the number of floors, the buildings were of the same height. The little girl was trying to jump above the grille that covered the wall, to catch a glimpse of her father. On the other end, standing outside courtroom no. 57, an equally jittery man was craning his neck to see her. He wanted to hold her in his arms, hug her. Nine years ago, when he was escorted into the police van, to be taken to court for the case hearing, his wife had held their newborn up for him to see. He hadn't been able to touch her; his hands were too big for the bars of the grille.

As the police started closing the windows on the third floor—they had noticed the father and daughter communicating via sign language—the girl ran down to the second floor of the old secretariat building. Her mother ran to catch up with her and to speak to her husband through the windows on the second floor. Tanveer explained the verdict to his wife. He gestured at her quickly—his hand slashing his throat, and then opening and closing his fist to show the number 'five'. Five of them had been sentenced to death.

Tanveer had escaped the gallows. Despite Special Public Prosecutor Raja Thakare demanding the death sentence for him, capital punishment had been given only to the five bomb planters arrested by the ATS. This did not mean Tanveer would walk scot-free; he was sentenced to life in prison. He tried to tell his daughter to take care of her mother, but the child didn't seem to understand and constantly tugged at her mother.

As their families were barred from the high-security public courtroom, this was the only way the accused could speak to their families. Families were not the only ones barred from setting foot in the fifth-floor courtroom. It had taken an intervention by the principal judge of the Sessions Court, Sangitrao Patil, for even journalists to be allowed inside.

During the nine-year trial, the families of the accused would spend the entire day with them in the court corridors, when they were brought there for the hearings. But after the judge pronounced them guilty, the same people weren't allowed to even come close to the convicts, for 'security reasons', forcing the kin of the accused to communicate through the windows on the other side.

~

11 September 2015

On a humid Wednesday afternoon, as a vintage clock on the white wall struck noon, Special Judge Y. D. Shinde, in the final verdict of his career—he was set to retire soon—found twelve of the thirteen accused guilty of perpetrating the 7/11 train blasts. The guilty included the bomb planters Kamal Ansari, Faisal Atta-ur Rahman Shaikh, Ehtesham Siddiqui, Naved Hussain Khan and Asif Bashir Khan, and the conspirators Tanveer Ansari, Mohammed Ali Alam Shaikh, Majid Shafi, Sajid Marghoob Ansari, Suhail Mehmood Shaikh and Zameer Latifur Rehman Shaikh.

It had taken the judge over a year to dictate the 1839-page judgement, summarizing over 16,000 pages of evidence, hundreds of applications, and nine years of twists, turns and controversies.

Final arguments in the case had ended on 19 August 2014. However, summons were issued to the jail officials the evening before the verdict, asking all the thirteen accused to be produced in the court the next day. The defence and prosecution, too, were told late in the evening that the verdict would be announced the next day. The date selected for the verdict was symbolic: 11 September 2015, exactly fourteen years after the attack on the World Trade Center in the United States.

The next morning the accused, the defence and prosecution lawyers reached court for the verdict. It all happened in a flash; the entire proceedings were over within ten minutes. In a single breath, in the presence of all the investigating officers from the ATS, now scattered across various postings, Judge Shinde asked the accused to stand up. One by one, each man listened as the judge read the charges for which the accused had been found guilty.

Only one man was acquitted—Abdul Wahideen Mohammad Shaikh, a secondary-school teacher with the Anjuman-i-Islam A.S.S. School. He had been accused of harbouring Pakistani bomb planters, but was acquitted of all charges. His lawyer, Prakash Shetty, immediately petitioned that his school be ordered to take him back, to regain his dignity. The request was declined.

Almost certain that the prosecution would demand the death sentence for those found guilty, the defence asked only for two things—a soft copy of the judgement and two weeks' time to argue the sentence that should be awarded. Both their requests were denied. The defence bowed their heads in despair. Rejections of applications were not uncommon, but this time Advocate Sharif Shaikh, part of the defence team and the most polite of all the lawyers, was appalled. 'An entire year to dictate the judgement, but not even two weeks' time to prepare a final appeal,' he muttered. The court was adjourned for arguments from both sides, before the final sentence on 30 September. There was no drama, no tears, nothing. The accused, now the guilty, were escorted out of court from a separate exit, as discreetly as they had been brought in.

It was unusual that news of the verdict in a major case was not reported instantaneously. But as journalists weren't allowed inside the court, they had to wait for former ATS chief K.P. Raghuvanshi to break the news to them. Journalists, with their cameras and mics, were quick to surround Raghuvanshi, hanging on to his every word. Before basking in those few minutes of fame, Raghuvanshi, dressed in an ink-blue shirt, his dark-brown-coloured hair dye fading, embraced every one of his ten investigators, congratulating them for securing a conviction. The families of the accused were waiting in the building opposite and were the last ones to hear of the verdict.

After the adjournment, the first phone call Khan, who represented five of the guilty, made was to Yug Mohit Chaudhry. He was in Jalna at that time and Khan asked him to return as soon as possible. Chaudhry had been a force to reckon with in the case and had been part of its most crucial arguments in court. He had argued the defence's strongest alibi, their CDRs.

From the quality of the evidence on record, he strongly believed that the men he was arguing for were innocent. Chaudhry wasn't one to dwell on his emotions. He would distance himself from the personalities involved in the case and believed, like any intelligent lawyer, only in the facts on record. Yet, there were certain things that Chaudhry would not tolerate. At the top of that list were human rights violations and breaches of the sanctity of the judicial system. His arguments against the death penalty were not only legally sound but also extremely passionate.

It had been two days since the verdict. While people across the country switched on their television sets, wondering if the convicts would be awarded the death penalty, the entire defence team was fighting tooth and nail to save the twelve men from the noose. Chaudhry's plans were elaborate. They began by broaching the death penalty law in India, citing a landmark judgement by the Supreme Court—Bachan Singh v/s State of Punjab. In that case, though the Supreme Court upheld the constitutional validity of the death penalty, it was the first time the formula which reserves the death penalty for the 'rarest of rare' cases was introduced.

The procedure for determining whether a case falls under this category involves preparation of a balance sheet of the aggravating and mitigating circumstances under which the act was committed. In such cases, life imprisonment was to be the rule and the death penalty an exception to the rule, only to be used in extremely rare circumstances.

Despite the judge's visible reluctance, Chaudhry argued that based on the law, before a person is sentenced to death, the court must arrive at the conclusion that there is no room for reform based on 'hard evidence'.

According to Chaudhry, the probation officer's report would serve as the best record of the time the accused spent in jail over the past nine years. 'What better evidence than the report of a qualified officer, a government employee, to ascertain if there is any chance of reformation?' he argued in court.

He also emphasized the fact that the role played by a person in a crime is of utmost importance. He said that even according to the police, in the present case, the accused were nothing more than foot soldiers, brainwashed by the LeT. Quoting ATS reports, he said that the accused had been repeatedly indoctrinated to 'avenge the atrocities' committed against Indian Muslims; they were mere 'pawns' in the hands of Azam Cheema.

Two volumes of written arguments and forty-three judgements substantiated Chaudhry's arguments. In a last-ditch attempt for leniency, and for the first time in the history of Maharashtra courts, the defence called in witnesses, ranging from the jail teacher to relatives of the accused, on the point of reform. Each examination aimed to demonstrate that the accused had become changed men over the years, with most of them enrolling in IGNOU courses and helping other prisoners, thinking they had their entire lives ahead of them. They had believed that the evidence adduced by the prosecution was not enough to punish them. How, then, could they be sentenced to death?

A report by the Law Commission of India, released on 15 August 2015, showed that the Supreme Court had confirmed the sentence in only 4.3 per cent cases involving the death penalty. In other words, in a staggering 95.7 per cent of such cases the trial courts had erroneously invoked the death penalty. The same commission, however, recommended that the death penalty be abolished for all offences barring cases of terrorism.

It was now Thakare's turn to put his best foot forward. In its closing arguments on the quantum of sentence, the prosecution sought the death penalty for eight of the twelve convicted, sparing the other four. Thakare reiterated the damage—both monetary and human—sustained from the blasts. 'If they are merchants of death,' he declared, 'then why should an honest taxpayer pay for the upkeep and maintenance of such unworthy people? Why should they be burdened with maintaining them at all?' There was a loud gasp from the dock where the accused were seated. He dismissed the defence's contention that the twelve men had families to take care of. 'At the time of committing the crime, you did not think of this. Now you are worried about what will happen to your family?' he said sharply.

Nevertheless, Thakare did not want to be perceived as hungry for their blood. He stressed that he was not seeking the death penalty for all the convicts. While he sought the death penalty for eight convicts, he asked for life imprisonment until the end of their natural lives for the other four convicts. The grim line on the prosecutor's face said it all—their crime was unforgivable.

'It is common knowledge that the suburban trains from Churchgate to Virar are always crowded and during peak hours they are jam-packed,' Thakare said. There was no need for him to point out what was chillingly obvious to the rest of the courtroom—a bomb blast in such a train was bound to cause maximum damage. The calculated selection of the targets was evidence of the convicts' 'extreme mentality', he claimed. He ended his submissions by declaring 'they are incapable of reform.'

Later, in his judgement on 30 September, Judge Shinde would end up echoing Thakare's arguments. He dismissed every single submission made by the accused as either stereotypical or non-applicable. The sheer scale of damage to human life was too costly to pardon them. All doors of hope of life imprisonment were closed.

On 30 September, the names of the five planters were read out again—Kamal Ansari, Faisal Atta-ur Rehman Shaikh, Ehtesham Siddiqui, Naved Hussain Khan and Asif Bashir Khan. They were sitting at the back, in the dock meant for the accused. As their names were called out, they stood up. The sections under which they were charged and convicted were read out. They were charged for murder and conspiracy, under sections of the Explosive Substances Act, the MCOCA and the Indian Penal Code.

All five were given the capital punishment. The judge fined all of them for each violated section of the law. The total fine was a staggering Rs 2,15,40,000. In most cases, those accused would scream, weep and lose control over themselves as the verdict was passed. But the twelve men sitting in the dock that day remained quiet and composed. Naved believed that his place within the four walls of the prison or outside of it was predestined. He had already accepted the judgement as part of his destiny and tried to bring some cheer in the dock by imitating one of his co-accused.

As though in a rush, the judge called out the names of the remaining convicts and read out the sections under which they were found guilty, before sentencing them to serve life imprisonment.

Two days after the sentencing, Atta-ur Rahman, Faisal and Muzzammil's father, suffered a massive heart attack. With one son sentenced to death, the other to a life in prison and the third, and the smartest of them all, Rahil, still absconding, he was a shattered man.

Later, in his judgement, Judge Shinde would reason why he was sentencing some to death and others to life imprisonment.

It is clear that the nature of the mitigating circumstances claimed by all the accused are not sufficient to overlook the aggravating circumstances. This case is, without a doubt, rarest of the rare. These accused are not hardened criminals—in the sense that they are not criminals whose livelihood is crime. They are terrorists with a particular mindset and followers of an ideology adverse to society and democratically established government.

To show leniency or mercy in the case of crimes of such magnitude, where the accused have shown no repentance or remorse after exhibiting an extremely depraved mentality, would be a travesty of justice.

The court owes justice not only to the accused, but also to the victims and society at large. Therefore, it is the duty of a court to award the proper sentence in view of the nature of offence and the manner in which it was executed. To expect society to be a silent spectator to this kind of depraved behaviour, to continue to extend its protective arm to the convicts, would be both unnatural and ridiculous.

In his judgement, Judge Shinde quoted the Chinese philosopher Confucius, 'If justice goes astray, the people will stand about in helpless confusion.' He also cited in his judgement an article in a *Times of India* publication, *The Speaking Tree*, dated 9 November 2014, written by Islamic scholar Maulana Wahiduddin Khan. The essay was in connection with the deadly attack that had taken place on 2 November 2014, in Wagah, Pakistan.

Maulana Khan appealed to the terrorists to come out of their primitive, violent mindsets through education and find peaceful ways to vent their anger. He wrote about the deadly attack, and questioned why news originating from Muslim countries was of a violent nature:

> Obviously, the purpose of this violence is to achieve some goal. But, whatever be the goal, the violent method has become quite irrelevant in present times . . . Now we are living in the age of freedom and science. Now, the peaceful approach is far more effective than violence.
>
> According to my experience, the solution to the problem of violence lies in education. The greatest problem with a large section of the Muslim community is that its members are lagging behind in modern, scientific education. It is modern education alone that can change traditional mindsets . . . Countering the problem with the gun cannot make those who are engaged in violence abandon their violent ways . . .
>
> There is the widespread notion that Islam promotes violence . . . [And] some Muslims are engaged in militancy in the name of Islam . . . The problem is that under the influence of certain thinkers, some Muslims have come to believe in the concept of establishing an Islamic system . . . For this, they require political power. But when they set out to establish this system, they see that a group is already

occupying the political seat. So, they try to overthrow or unseat those who are in possession of political power . . . This thinking is completely un-Islamic, because Islam enjoins on its followers to follow its teachings at the individual level, rather than foisting them on others by force or violence.

The target of religion, including Islam, is to bring about reform in the individual and not in the political system. Any kind of spiritual or intellectual change can be brought about in an individual only when he is addressed peacefully . . . There is a prophetic saying that some Muslims will indulge in un-Islamic activities in their later generations. The Prophet was asked how this would happen. The Prophet answered that they would give Islamic names to non-Islamic activities. What is wrong with them is that they have given the name of jihad to their militancy to seek justification for their terror activities. The need of the hour is to correct this self-styled interpretation of Islam and then everything will fall into place.

20

Volte-face

A decade ago, four bombs hit Malegaon on the holy day of Shab-e-Baraat, scarring the city's inhabitants, 86 per cent of whom are Muslim, both physically and mentally. The first suspects in the ATS investigation were Muslims and residents of Malegaon wondered why the police assumed that Muslims were responsible for the blasts. Why would they target their own community, near a mosque?

The court's order on 27 April 2016 ended that particular line of investigation. Judge V.V. Patil, of the special National Investigation Agency court, concluded that there was not enough evidence to prosecute the eight men arrested. The ninth one, Shabbir Masiullah, had died a year ago, waiting to be cleared of all charges. The court found the ATS's theory unbelievable—that a group of Muslims would decide to kill 'their own people' to create disharmony between two communities. Ganesh *visarjan* was just days before Shab-e-Baraat. The court observed that if these men really wanted to stoke communal fires, they would have bombed the visarjan to ensure maximum Hindu casualties. The men were scapegoats in the ATS's investigation, the judge remarked in the discharge order. Though the ATS theory was mocked in court, the investigating agency wasn't censured for its shoddy investigation because of a 'lack of intent'.

This verdict indirectly acknowledged the possibility of a Hindu terrorist organization's hand behind the blasts.

Except a few officers, the same team investigated the 7/11 blasts case, the Malegaon blasts and the Aurangabad arms haul case. There were unnerving similarities between the Malegaon investigation, now termed inaccurate, and the 7/11 probe. Like in the 7/11 case, where eleven out of the thirteen accused 'confessed', seven out of the nine accused 'confessed' to the Malegaon blasts. The way these confessions were recorded too was similar—they were in Hindi and not in Urdu, their mother tongue, an eyewitness claimed he had seen Pakistanis making the bombs along with Mohammed Ali and Asif, the police seized SIMI literature and found RDX traces months later.

The ATS's original case in the Malegaon blasts hinged on the 'confessions', where the accused allegedly claimed that they harboured Pakistanis and made the bombs a month before the blasts. When the National Investigation Agency (NIA) traced all the witnesses, a can of worms was opened. One of them, an eyewitness to the bomb making, said he was pressurized by the ATS to make the statement.

The ATS had used two panch witnesses to show that the traces of explosives found in the soil samples from the blast sites matched the explosives found in soil at Shabbir Masiullah's battery unit. The ATS claimed to have found RDX in one sample out of the four taken from each corner of Masiullah's godown. However, both witnesses said that they were not present in the godown when the samples were collected. The NIA found something else that further blew open the ATS's case. On 1 August, more than a month before the 8 September blasts, Masiullah was already in the custody of the Mumbai Crime Branch. The ATS alleged that Masiullah was a key conspirator and had procured the explosive material from Mumbai with the help of Mohammed Ali and Asif. According to the ATS, the bombs were made four days before his detention on 8 August. Why then did the ATS and the Crime Branch not find the bombs when Masiullah was arrested? How was the plan executed without him, the key conspirator?

Another prime accused in the case was Zahid Majid Ansari. Ansari, now a fodder and firewood seller, was accused of planting one of the bombs. However, on the day of the blasts, he was in Fulsawangi district in Yavatmal, 400 kilometres from the blast site, where he taught in a madrasa. He even attended the evening namaz in Fulsawangi. According to the NIA, Ansari had been seen by at least twelve people in Yavatmal that day.

The ATS had two witnesses for the fake bombs recovered from Mohammedia Masjid. The time of recovery of the bombs was between 12.15 p.m. and 8 p.m. on 13 September 2006, according to police records. But one of the witnesses had signed the panchnama when the clothes of the blast victims were allegedly seized at 4.30p.m. the same day. How could the same person be at two places at the same time?

Within a year of the blasts, the people of Malegaon had filed over a hundred affidavits in various courts, all stating that the arrested men were innocent. But it was only the sensational confession by Swami Aseemanand that raised questions about the ATS's investigation. By then, the accused had already spent five and a half years in prison. In 2011, when the investigation passed from the ATS to the NIA, the NIA absolved the eight men and accused Hindu extremists instead—Manohar Narwaria, Rajendra Chaudhary, Dhan Singh, Shiv Singh, Lokesh Sharma, Sunil Joshi (who had passed away by then) and the wanted accused—Ramchandra Kalsangra, Ramesh Venkat Mahalkar and Sandeep Dange.

Even after the NIA submitted a charge sheet against the Hindu accused, charging them for carrying out the blasts, the discharge of the originally arrested Muslim accused was not proposed. Their case was heard in the same court as the 7/11 blasts case and, even after the men themselves filed for discharge, their application was not heard. Judge Shinde had said that he was busy with the 7/11 blasts case. Much later, a different judge was assigned for this case, paving the way for a hearing on their application.

The lawyers of the Hindu accused insisted that the ATS come to court and defend their stand. Everyone expected a war of words between the NIA and ATS in court. Instead, the NIA changed tack or did an 'ulta face' (volte-face), as the judge phrased it in his order. Even though the NIA now blamed a Hindu terror organization for the attacks, they recommended that the Muslim accused continue to remain in custody. They also demanded that the court weigh the evidence collected by both agencies and then make a judgement.

The NIA was represented in the Malegaon case by Advocate Prakash Shetty, who had defended Faisal along with four others in the 7/11 blasts case.

The accused sitting at the back of the courtroom could not understand what was happening. Was the NIA really against their release after the ATS's shoddy investigation was exposed? On the last day in court, it was a 3:1 fight—with the

NIA, ATS and the Hindu extremists on one side and the eight Muslim accused on the other.

The court finally decided in the favour of the Muslim accused. But it was a confusing night for Mohammed Ali and Asif; while one judge had branded them dreaded criminals, another court had declared them innocent.

21

The Blasts' Echo

It is said that moments before you die, your entire life flashes in front of your eyes. Thirty-year-old Ashwin Boricha knows this is true. When the bomb went off between Khar and Santacruz, he saw his life whizz right in front of his eyes. His chest and right thigh sustained deep wounds, his right eyeball popped out and the satchel he was carrying tore into his shoulder.

On 11 July 2006, everything went wrong for Boricha. As the stereo in his car was stolen, he took the train to work that day. He was asked not to come in, but decided to go anyway. 'That evening, when I was about to leave office, my boss asked me to stay back and get some work done. I told him I had to rush home to get the car fixed; he didn't really like it but let me go anyway. Today, he just wishes he had stopped me.'

Several severely injured blast victims fell unconscious after the blasts, only to open their eyes days later, but not this art director. He slipped into unconsciousness only for a few minutes. 'A human chain had been formed; I was brought on to the road and left there. The next thing I remember was being taken inside an autorickshaw. I was lying where passengers

189

keep their feet. My legs were hanging out from one side and my head from the other. I kept curling up, fearing I would lose my head. It was the most torturous ride of my life. The other victim in the rickshaw had cracked his skull, so he was wailing in pain throughout the ride and kept tugging at my hair. But in those moments, I didn't feel so much pain as much as the shock of it all.'

Boricha remembers that he was taken to Cooper Hospital and was kept alongside several others—most of whom were lying motionless. There were so many splinters all over his upper body that the doctors couldn't find a single clean area in which they could insert the injection. His eyelids, lips, eyes and nostrils were all torn, and his throat burnt like someone had set it on fire. There were no clothes left on his body, just their tatters hanging off him. The impact of the blast was so strong that the green paint from inside the coach was stuck to his body like glue.

'I remember I could not see from one eye and I could not hear very well. I cried out for help after which I was taken to the second floor of the hospital. I weighed some 70-odd kilograms then. I was dropped twice on the way up. When we finally reached, I noticed that someone had just breathed their last on a bed. So they put his body down and placed me on that bed . . . The doctor explained that there was no other option as there were so many injured.'

Boricha was immediately shifted to Criticare Hospital, a private medical set-up, where doctors performed a surgery on him and cleaned his body. The operation lasted more than four hours, as doctors meticulously removed the shrapnel, wood and cloth stuck on him. Even today, bits of shrapnel can still be found on his body. 'When my mother saw me, I knew she thought I wouldn't survive.' Every time there is some news about the blasts, the story of his survival is recounted in the Boricha household. Ashwin has thirty-two stitches on his body, he is blind in one eye and has lost 30 per cent of his hearing.

After surgery in Criticare Hospital, Boricha was taken to Bombay Hospital where he stayed in the ICU for around four days. For three months, he was bedridden; every nightmare he had would involve the blast.

He may have survived, but the incident took a toll on him—financially and physically. When Boricha as much as sneezes, his whole body aches. Staying in a bungalow in Gorai, the commute from Borivali to town was very difficult for him. Boricha was left with no option but to use a cab to travel once he rejoined work. 'The railways was absolutely apathetic to our plight. It was such a futile exercise for us injured to come in four to five times to get the entire claim amount from the tribunal. We would be made to sit for hours and sent back if a single document was missing. It was humiliating,' Boricha recalls. However, he praised the ATS for being considerate enough to send someone to pick up and drop the victims back, whenever they were required in the office. The agency was extremely disappointed when very few people actually turned up to testify in court. 'It was just me and two other senior citizens from my compartment who went to court.'

A year after the blast, Boricha took the same train and travelled in the same compartment in a bid to confront his fears. In the years that passed, despite the immense care he required, Boricha travelled as much as he could, mostly for work. He slowly started driving his car and bike again. He took up photography and scriptwriting—both of which aided his work. But he has accepted that his dream of becoming a creative head may never be fulfilled. Two years ago, everything came to a standstill when the company he was working for downsized and he lost his job.

'Now no one seems keen on hiring a one-eyed art director with damaged hearing,' he rues.

~

'Aai,' a frail man, lying on bed number twenty-seven on the eighth floor of Hinduja Hospital, whispered as he attempted to speak for the first time in two years. Crippled after being severely injured in the blast near Mira Road, Parag Sawant's first word brought a smile to his mother, Madhuri's, face. It was the day of Diwali in 2008, Madhuri reminisces. Her son had been left comatose after sustaining grievous injuries in the blast. Though he had recovered consciousness after several months of intensive treatment, he was in a vegetative state.

Today, he moved his lips slowly, carefully, much like a child learning to speak. Madhuri rushed to find the doctors, lest someone accused her of hallucinating. Her eyes welled up when doctors confirmed that Parag was, in fact, trying to speak. His most special visitor that day was his two-year-old daughter, Prachiti, whom he had never met before. She was a perfect mix of both her parents. He could not move, so he just lay there gaping at her in wonder.

From nurses to doctors, everyone spoke about Parag's determination to live. News channels began profiling him, and politicians, like Union Minister Sushma Swaraj and Deputy Prime Minister L.K. Advani, dropped into the hospital to pay him a visit. It was as if Mumbai wanted Parag to be the success story that parents would tell their kids for generations to come.

In the months that followed, a speech therapist, a physiotherapist and his neurosurgeon visited him almost daily.

Parag Sawant was a survivor. There wasn't a single day he was left alone. Someone from his family, mostly his mother, would sit by his side. She made it a point to kiss his forehead before she left every evening. Parag, with his extreme brain damage, would just stare at her, motionless. But his mother knew how her son liked things clean and ensured that everything, from his clothes to his hair, was spick and span.

Parag's health slowly improved in the next few months. He moved his finger one day, closed his fist another day, blinked his eyes the next. He would remember and then forget things. And then, after months of treatment and therapy, he was able to sit up in the bed, leaning against the backrest. His mother, his father, Jayprakash, who worked as a welder at Mazgaon Dock, and his wife, Preeti, never lost hope.

But then there were those convulsions that would send him back into coma. He would slip into unconsciousness and then wake up again after many hours. These long blackouts, doctors said, indicated how grave the injuries really were. Two years later, in 2010, he slipped back into coma, and did not wake up again. His family refused to give up. 'He was my son; how could we leave him just like that? We meant the world to him and he to us. A single occasion didn't pass without him gifting everyone something. I always wore the saris he gifted me, whether it was for Mother's Day or Diwali,' Madhuri recalls. She travelled 34 kilometres each morning to take care of him; sometimes going back home in the same train Parag boarded that fateful day.

Her son was obedient, never the kind to trouble her and he loved playing kabaddi.

'When Parag was injured in the blast,' says Madhuri, 'Preeti was heavily pregnant and was resting at home. A few children playing within the compound guided a stranger, holding Parag's identity card, to our house. I didn't want to hear what he had to say.' The family lived in the Ramabai Co-operative Housing Society in Bhayander. She remembers the phone lines were down that day. Parag worked as an assistant manager for an Andheri-based builder. He had told his mother that morning that he would try to come home early, so they could discuss his wife's *godh bharai* (a Maharashtrian ceremony performed in the seventh month of pregnancy for the unborn baby). 'He wanted to get the house painted before that,' she recalls.

Parag was first taken to Bhakti Vedanta Hospital in Mira Road, but by the time he was transferred to Hinduja Hospital the next day, he had already slipped into coma. The first sign indicating that his vital organs were failing was when he became breathless, with his oxygen saturation levels decreasing alarmingly. At 6.54 a.m. on 7 July 2015, he succumbed to a cardio-respiratory attack. He was thirty-six years old. When he went back home, nine years later, he was in a casket. Scores of people from the vicinity and the media surrounded his family. The last man, the 189th victim of the 7/11 blasts, was laid to rest just four days before the ninth anniversary of the terror strike. Madhuri doesn't have to travel the 34 kilometres any more. She now spends her time looking after the house and her granddaughter, a student of class four. The girl could never hug her father or sleep on his lap or demand a vacation from him. She could only see him lying in a hospital bed, motionless. 'I take walks in the evening, spending time with my granddaughter. The doctor insists on these walks. I miss my son every single day.'

Two months after Parag breathed his last, the Sawants were glued to the television set as the verdict was announced. Nearly a year after the blasts, the railways had offered Parag's wife, Preeti, a job. While Madhuri took care of Parag in hospital, Preeti cleared her class twelve exams. She had only recently left her job with a private firm, when she came to know she was pregnant. Since her father-in-law retired in 2010, she is the only breadwinner of the house.

She sits at the ticket counter at Bhayander station, counting her days. Madhuri insists that no one talk to Preeti about Parag's fight for survival. 'She will start crying. If you dwell on the past, you end up staying there for days,' she says. The Sawants haven't celebrated a single festival since Parag's death.

~

A lime and three chillies, an Indian superstition meant to keep the evil eye at bay, hangs on the iron door that leads to the Kotian household, on the third floor of the Sai Dham Tower, in distant Nalasopara.

At first glance, Balkrishna looks completely fine. Tall and fair-skinned, he stands up to greet us. But a closer look reveals his scars—he has a deep one around his wrist that spreads all the way up to his forearm, one on his face and another one on his balding head. When asked about these scars, the forty-five-year-old man sits in silence for a full minute. We repeat our question, but Kotian continues staring at us. Only after a few minutes does realization dawn upon us—Kotian's eardrums were severely damaged in the blasts and he is almost deaf.

He cringes when we speak extra loudly for his benefit, but understands the question. We gesture more prominently through the remainder of the conversation to communicate better with him. Since the blast, Kotian has not heard the sounds of the ducks playing in his society's pond or enjoyed the Ganpati festival when crowds dance to drum beats. Loud noises hurt his ears.

As many as 70 per cent of those who survived the blasts suffered from loss of hearing, but Kotian was among the few rendered almost completely deaf. On that fateful day, just like any other day, Kotian took the 6.15 p.m. train from Bombay Central station. He worked as a dental lab technician in the area. When the bomb went off near Jogeshwari, splinters pierced his ears and the sound of the explosion rendered him partially deaf. Splinters also entered Kotian's head and a rod hit him on his wrist. 'My time was "right", the watch on my right wrist stopped my hand from being dismembered from the forearm,' he says.

For more than a month, Kotian was on bed rest. For four more months he couldn't move out of his house. Eight months after the blasts, he underwent an ear surgery at Alliance Hospital. Though every surgery was said to be successful, it didn't bring back his hearing. He didn't have the luxury of time. It had been only six months since he had purchased his house on loan and his son was only eight months old while his daughter was three. Who was going to repay the loan and fend for his children if he kept going back to the hospital?

To explain his trauma and the injuries he sustained, Kotian hands over his thick medical file. This way, he is spared the pain of deciphering what we ask. 'My hands used to shake slightly at work, but they all put up with me,' he says, the agony visible in his eyes. For the next seven years, every single day, Kotian took the same train that almost killed him. He didn't have a choice, just like several others. What helped him survive was the determination of his wife, Jayshree, and his brother and sister.

In 2015, after saving some money, Kotian quit his job and set up a small laboratory close to his house. He now works even during the vacations, when his wife and children go to their village. He smiles when he sees his children playing with the ducks in his building's compound.

~

Chirag Chauhan's story is an inspirational one. His is the story of a city's determination to get back on its feet. It doesn't matter if the blasts paralysed him from the waist down.

He smiles throughout the conversation, even though he is talking about the biggest tragedy of his life. Chirag now drives a golden-coloured Hyundai i10, which is modified to suit his handicap. Seated on a wheelchair behind a desk in his 200 square-foot office in Mahavir Nagar, Kandivali, Chirag is frantically trying to meet the year-end deadline in his small chartered accountancy firm. The only thing different about him, apart from the obvious disability, is the weight he has put on in the past ten years. In 2015, he started an online portal for all types of professional services, including lawyers and chartered accountants.

Chirag continues to live with a splinter, the size of a bullet, that pierced his spinal cord during the blasts. He is not bitter about his wounds, and has chosen to live with a certain calm and lots of laughter. But his sixty-three-year-old mother, Anjana, still finds it difficult to hold back her tears when she thinks of the past. She insists that her son has never cried in the last ten years. 'Of course I cry, I just don't do it in front of her. I know how difficult it is for her to just see me this way,' says Chirag.

Chirag, the youngest of four siblings, was only twenty-one at the time of the blasts; he had just graduated that year. With two of his older sisters married, he lived with his mother and third sister, Kavita. Chirag's father, a manager with Hindustan

Petroleum, had passed away when Chirag was eighteen years old, due to kidney failure. An aspiring chartered accountant, Chirag was doing his articleship with A.J. Shah in south Mumbai. He had only recently purchased the first-class monthly pass and started travelling by train to work. Until then, he drove around on his black Kinetic scooter—it was the last gift his father had given him.

Chirag usually left work at 7 p.m., but that day his sister Kavita wanted to go out in the evening, so he left early. Suddenly, between Khar and Santacruz, a bomb ripped through his train compartment. Not realizing that it was a bomb blast, Chirag first thought the train had derailed. At home, his mother and sister frantically tried calling up his cell phone. 'We had just returned from our evening prayers when our neighbours came running and asked us to put on the television. The carnage was bloody. So when I couldn't get through to my son, I just knew something really bad had happened,' Chirag's mother said.

Chirag didn't lose consciousness immediately. 'I couldn't feel anything waist down. People carried me to the hospital. After going from one hospital to another, I was finally taken to KEM . . . I don't remember what happened after that.' For the next few days, Girivar Apartments in Kandivali had a steady stream of visitors through the day, praying for the young man's recovery.

Chirag was discharged after two and a half months. Initially, doctors were doubtful if he would even be able to sit up by himself. 'The doctor was very clear that exercise was extremely important [for his recovery]. It started with eight hours of exercise a day, then six and now, finally, it has reduced to an hour a day,' he says. Chirag doesn't want to take revenge on the men who did this to him, but he believes everyone gets their due in the end. 'I remember lying in bed and my best friends were quarrelling about who would get my Scooty, just to tease me. During our college days, I would not allow any one of them to even touch it.'

In 2009, with the help of his senior Nandita Parekh at the firm A.J. Shah, and with his best friends, Amish Parekh and Dharmesh Jain, by his side, Chirag cleared the chartered accountancy exam. Refusing to sit at home, he and an attendant would travel all the way to Chembur, for his work in Deloitte, a well-known financial services firm. But as the monsoons loomed, the risk of venturing out with a handicap set in. He finally started his own firm in 2012 and now supports his mother financially. His sister had initially refused to get married as she did not want to leave her mother alone; however, she agreed to get married a few years ago and now lives in the United States.

'I have everything I want and will ever need.' Chirag doesn't mention the fever and infection he gets every month due to sitting continuously on his black-coloured wheelchair. 'I will stand someday,' he says quietly.

In an email to us, he once quoted Winston Churchill, 'Success is not final, failure is not fatal; it is the courage to continue that counts.'

The black Scooty, parked in the garage, still awaits its rider.

~

Prashant Rathi, twenty-eight, was on his way from Lower Parel to attend an ISKCON meeting in Malad on 11 July 2006. Sitting in the first-class compartment of the train, he dozed off while chanting prayers under his breath. Suddenly, a loud noise startled him out of his nap. Has the train derailed, he asked himself. Opening his eyes, he noticed the train was motionless on the tracks between Khar and Santacruz stations. He looked around only to realize there had been an explosion in the train.

Rathi still held the rosary bag in his hand, but the beads were nowhere to be seen. His shirt had ripped open and his trousers were torn below the knees. The office mobile phone in his shirt pocket and his office bag were missing. When he looked towards the window, one seat away from him, he saw that the skeleton of the compartment of the train had been torn apart by the intensity of the explosion. He was surrounded by bodies, one of them lying opposite his seat. He was one of the very few people still alive in his compartment.

He heard a faint voice repeating the word 'help' near him. It was the man lying near his legs, who had fallen over a dead body. Rathi's ears were bleeding and he was starting to feel dizzy. He couldn't hear the sounds around him clearly. His hands, legs, back and face were all injured. He tried moving and with difficulty, he was able to extricate himself from the body lying on top of him. He turned the injured man over and noticed he was bleeding. The man's fingers had been cut off, and Rathi could see the nerves and veins hanging out from the open wound.

Rathi was horrified; he had never seen anything like this before. But when the injured man continued to cry for help, Rathi swallowed his fear and tried to lift him up. But the man was too heavy for the injured Rathi to carry out to safety. He exited the train and told the rescuers outside about the injured man inside.

A twist of fate saved Rathi's life that day. When he had boarded the crowded train, there was no place left to sit. He had tried to stand between two seats. 'Abhi aur kitna andar jaaun? (How much more should I move in?)' the man already standing there had said to him, irritated. When more people entered the train at the next station, another man asked Rathi to move deeper into the narrow passage area, near a different seat. Two more stations passed and Rathi found an empty seat. The bomb was placed on the luggage rack near the seats he had first stood next to.

Outside the train, Rathi miraculously found his rosary beads on the railway tracks, not damaged by the explosion. The police also found his office bag and his mobile phone the next day. He was most worried about the fate of his siblings and father, all of whom used to commute by local trains and would have definitely been in different trains at that point in time. But Rathi, a very religious man, was hopeful and put his faith in Sri Sri Radha Gopinathji, believed to be a form of Krishna. He prayed while he made his way back home through the pouring rain and incessant traffic.

The family itself was incredibly fortunate. Rathi's brother and sister were on the train in which the bomb went off near Bandra, but they were in another compartment. His father wasn't as lucky as his children. He had been in the same compartment as the bomb that exploded at Mahim station. He had injured his head, forearm and back, and ruptured both eardrums. Responders rushed him to Hinduja Hospital where he regained consciousness.

'We all were saved by the merciful glance of the lord upon us,' Rathi later remarked. He believes he was saved by the prayers of his fellow devotees. This experience has reaffirmed Rathi's faith in Krishna. He got married soon after the blasts and now tries to be more conscious of Krishna every day of his life.

～

On 20 April 2016, we walked into Churchgate railway station, the southern terminus of the Western Railway line. There were CCTV cameras everywhere, including inside a few compartments. Every station had a help desk manned by at least three constables in case of an emergency. However, only one of the three entrances had a body scanner. Ironically, the first CCTV camera was set up just a day after the blasts. In the ladies' compartment, an announcement reminds us of the danger that will always persist. 'Check beneath your seat for suspicious objects,' the voice says clearly. Mumbai's railway line will always remain a soft target.

22

'My Acquittal Defeats the ATS'

Of the thirteen men accused for planning and executing the 7/11 train blasts, only one man was acquitted on 11 September 2015. When Abdul Wahideen Mohammad Shaikh, a schoolteacher by profession, finally walked out of prison the next day, he marvelled at how much the world had changed. So many more skyscrapers and skywalks, a new metro network and monorail, all waited to greet him as he tried to put nine years of prison behind him. His two children eagerly waited for their *abbu* to come home and take them out somewhere . . . an outing where they would explore the changed Mumbai city together. Here is his story in his own words:

> For the past nine years, my wife, Sajida, would tell my children, Umar, eleven, and Umrah, ten, that daddy will take you out once he is back home. When a man comes home after spending nine years in jail, freed of every charge, this is what is expected of him—that he will spend time with his family and enjoy the world with them. But even though I am back, I still can't do these things. I ask them

to wait for some more time and pacify them, but how long will this go on?

I am a teacher at the Anjuman-i-Islam A.S.S. School. I am thankful that I got my job back within twenty days of my acquittal. But, even though I have a job, I haven't been paid a dime since I joined.

A person who is released from jail and has been cleared of all charges always fears that the government will appeal against his release and confine him behind bars once again. There is a six-month period to file an appeal and that period is over now. But an Intelligence Bureau official told me that the period is actually three years. I suspect this was said to ensure I don't write about my experiences or talk too much to other people about everything I went through. When the IB officer meets me, he always tells me to forget the rest of them still in prison. He says he has put in a lot of effort to have me acquitted. He constantly tells me that the ATS has not won by convicting twelve men, but they lost by acquitting one.

My tussle with the law began a decade ago. I was not on very good terms with the president of the local mosque in Mumbra. I belong to the Ahle-Hadees sect. We don't wear skullcaps or believe in an Imam. We only believe in the Quran and Hadis—teachings of Mohammed Rasoolilah— unlike other Sunni Muslims. He didn't want me to pray in that mosque and was a supporter of the police. This was back in 1999. A police officer approached the president and told him they wanted to arrest some men who had been affiliated with SIMI, now that the organization was banned. This is how the first case was registered against me in 2001. After that, whenever there was a riot or a blast or any other law and order situation, I would be called into the police station. Even in this case [the 7/11 blasts], because of the SIMI case registered against me, I was called in for questioning, tortured even before I was officially arrested and eventually, I was falsely implicated. I often think about my days in police custody. For three months, I had to face third-degree torture. I was abused, stripped and beaten with a belt. I was forced to undergo water boarding—a technique where you are made to lie down, feet up, on a handcart, then your face is covered with a handkerchief. They put water up your nose through a pipeline. The cloth in between won't let you die, but it's difficult to remember that as you are being tortured. They threatened me with dire consequences and even disrespected Islam in front of me. That is when a man breaks.

Even though there was no evidence of my involvement in the blasts, and despite the directions of the Supreme Court and the Geneva Convention against torture, I was put through hell. I have said all of this under oath. I won't forget their names ever—ATS chief K.P. Raghuvanshi, Vasant Tajne, Arun Sambhaji Khanvilkar, Dinesh Kadam, Sachin Kadam, Kisan Shengal, B.B. Rathod, R.R. Joshi, Iqbal Shaikh and their juniors.

At first we [the thirteen accused] thought that there was some confusion and we would be released once the police realized we were innocent. Then, one day, we were told that we would be undergoing narco tests. We were very happy hearing this as we knew the truth—we were not involved in the blasts. Even the cops told us that we would be released if nothing was revealed in the test. But they lied to us.

When I think about my jail days, I can't forget how my daughter was even deprived of her mother's milk. My wife had to work since I was taken into custody. When I was brought to the court for the first time, my wife came to meet me. We had been married for only about three years when I was arrested. She was left to fend for herself and our children. She cried a lot when she learnt about the torture and arrest. She was also worried about our finances. She asked me if I would allow her to work. I didn't say yes or no, and left the decision to her.

She was always in a burqa; even my brothers had not seen her face until she started working a few days later.

I remained silent for a good five years in prison. I wouldn't talk to anyone. It was almost like a psychological disorder. I would meet the same set of people every day, follow the same routine in that small cell . . . It all started getting to me.

They would wake us up at 6 a.m. every day. After offering namaz, I would sit down with the other two inmates in my 8x8 ft cell. They would then open the gates at 7 a.m., after which we could go to the small open space outside where tea was served. I used to exercise for about an hour and would walk for close to four hours every day. Then, if you like, you can read the newspapers, some books or the Quran. Lunch would be served at 10 a.m.

The other accused and I used to sit around waiting to meet people. Every day we had hopes that someone would come to meet us or someone would just come and give us any news about the case. Maybe they would tell us when we would be released. It wasn't just the thirteen of us—every prisoner in jail lives in this hope. Deep down we knew that this was not likely, but we still lived in hope. At 4 p.m., we would be given dinner. Again, it was up to us if we wanted to save it for the night and eat it cold or eat the warm food then and there. By 5.30 p.m. we would be pushed back into our barracks.

After a point we did begin to wonder—how much namaz can one offer or how many books can one read? How much can we talk to each other? We could do this for one or two months, but for nine long years? We soon ran out of things to talk about. At times, we got depressed and cried. We used to ask ourselves just one question: why us and how did we land up in this mess? It was extremely painful for us.

All of us were counting days. Days turned into weeks and weeks into months. A year passed by. One day, a constable entered my barrack and said that my signature was required on my lawyer's vakalatnama. I was confused. We had already signed on our lawyer's vakalatnama. What was this new thing? We already had a lawyer fighting for us. The constable merely asked me to sign the papers. It was late in the evening and I did what I was told. The next day, my wife came to meet me in jail and told me that my father had passed away. The paper I had signed was to seek permission to attend the funeral. The funeral was organized for the very next day. I was taken to the kabristan and offered prayers for my father. That was a very painful experience for me.

My father used to tell me that with the SIMI tag attached to my name, the police harassment would never stop. He advised me to keep a low profile, and concentrate only on my family and my life. But he always stood beside me when the going got tough. He did say that one day the truth would be revealed. After my father's death, the relatives of many other co-accused too passed away. More than anything else, it was the helplessness we felt that hurt the most.

One day, I went up to an officer to tell him that Asif's father had passed away and that he needed to go for the funeral. The officer was surprised by my behaviour and asked me how I could be so normal while informing him about a death in someone's family. I replied that we were used to it by then.

I used to think that the cops inside prison and the ones outside were different, but I realized that they were exactly the same. When we went to Arthur Road Jail, Swati Sathe was the jail superintendent. She troubled us a lot and tried to force us to become approvers in the case. The entire team would enter the jail and pressurize us.

I have been saying this from the beginning—we are innocent. We underwent third-degree torture and confessions were extracted from us. We have been saying this in court from day one. Innumerable applications have been filed. But the court never believed us. The people actually involved in the blasts would not sit at home; they would have left the country by now. Many of the other accused—for instance, Mohammed Ali, Tanveer and my brother-in-law, Sajid—were regulars in police stations, like me. We would be pulled up for absolutely any crime that had been committed. If we were the real accused, we would never have gone to the police station voluntarily that day.

The ATS knew that their witnesses could potentially back out and so they wanted us to become approvers. They used every trick in the book. When their threats did not have any effect on me, they even attempted to bribe me with Rs 25 lakh, stating that I could take the money and set up a business and maybe even get my sister married. But when I refused this bribe, the torture only became worse.

One of my co-accused, Naved Hussain Khan, is a modern guy and he is quite fashionable. The police tried to turn him into an approver, but he also refused. Today twelve people have been convicted, but not one of them turned an approver. I am thankful to god for that. Witnesses can lie, the taxi drivers or panch witnesses can lie, but one accused turning into an approver would mean something different. I was acquitted because my relative didn't testify against me.

I got married in 2003. My brother-in-law, that is my wife's sister's husband, Mehmood, was also detained in the case. Before 2003, I did not know him. We became close after my marriage. He was tortured and his confession [statement] was recorded under Section 164 of the Code of Criminal Procedure, 1973. He was made to sign the statement in which he claimed I knew Ehtesham. I stay in Mumbra. My wife suffers a thyroid ailment and her doctor's office is in Vikhroli. So whenever I went to Vikhroli, I would hand over the keys to Mehmood. The ATS tried to make him claim that I instructed him that one man called Ehtesham would come to my house with his friends and that he should hand over the keys of the house to him. The ATS asked him to testify that Ehtesham and his friends had two meetings in my house. In the first meeting, the conspiracy was hatched and in the second meeting, they claimed that the Pakistanis had come and stayed in my house. Ehtesham's confession statement mentioned the same thing too. Mehmood was terrified and did not want any more trouble. The cops were arresting Muslims randomly and accusing them in false cases. So, out of fear, he complied and made that statement. After seven years, in the course of the trial, he retracted the statement. He gathered the courage to tell the court that the statement was fabricated and he never knew any

Ehtesham. He told the court that all the allegations against me were false and described how the ATS pressurized him to give the statement. Thankfully, after this, I was acquitted.

I would like to say that I am happy after I was released and that I am a free man now. But whenever I see or think about the other accused, I feel sad. I wonder what will happen to them and if any of them is given the death penalty, I feel that I will also die with them. They may be in captivity, but at least they are alive. I will do whatever I can to help them out.

Maps were allegedly found in the houses of the accused and the court accepted this claim. They found maps of Mumbai and Asia. The Mumbai map had important places marked on it and the Asia map had a route traced on it from Mumbai to Tehran and from Tehran to Pakistan. In today's day and age, where everyone uses the Internet and GPS, how could the court just accept the police claims of a physical map being found?

I studied a lot during my time in jail. I took up a course in journalism and a Master of Arts among other things. I am a teacher and I was always viewed with respect, yet I was harassed by the police. They have this hatred towards people accused in terror cases. Whether he is innocent or not, it doesn't matter to them. They just hate him and would do anything to harass him. They used to say that were I not accused in a terror case, I could have been useful by doing odd jobs around the jail—like looking after some paperwork, some staff duty or even teaching their kids.

After my release, my best moment was when I was called to the Tata Institute of Social Sciences to deliver a lecture on my experiences in jail. No one can ever return these nine years of my life. The torture I have gone through, the bad times . . . nothing can undo any of it. Many accused in the Aurangabad arms hauls case too, despite being released on bail, have found very little acceptance in society. No one gives you a job; you don't even have a place to live . . . [sometimes I think] it's easier to be submissive and stay inside the confines of prison than face the world outside.

My struggles aren't over yet. I have not been able to sleep or rest properly for days together. I am doing the best I can to ensure the other accused too are released, even if it means knocking on the doors of the Supreme Court. I know they are innocent; this is my contribution for their future.

While in the Arthur Road Jail I used the time to write a book about my experiences. An accused in the 1993 Mumbai blasts, Mustafa Dossa, helped me. The working title of my book is *The 7/11 Train Blasts*.

Allegations of torture against the police officers, including the then jail superintendent, have been made by the accused under oath. They have also stated that their confessions were recorded under duress and that the jail authorities tried very hard to turn them into approvers. The court has, however, discarded this contention of the accused, while accepting everything else stated in the confessions.

Epilogue

Every few months, Atta-ur Rahman Shaikh is abruptly woken up from his afternoon siesta. He can usually tell who is at the door, depending on how frantic the knocks are. Ten years ago, the police had charged each of Shaikh's three sons for their involvement in the 7/11 Mumbai train blasts. Faisal and Muzzammil were arrested, while Rahil was marked 'absconding'. Ever since, their father has been subjected to follow-up visits by the investigators, looking for the slightest of leads in their hunt.

The sixty-year-old, who sported a long white beard, frowned as the sunlight hit his face. This wasn't a constable who had visited him before. But in the satellite town of Mira Road, you only have to ask to find the house of Faisal Shaikh, arguably the most high profile of those accused in the case.

'*Main* police station *se aaya hoon*,' the visitor introduced himself. '*Batado* Rahil *kahan hai*. (I have come from the police station. Tell me where Rahil is).'

He wasn't the only one grappling with unanswered questions that rankle the 7/11 investigations. 'I don't know,' said Shaikh earnestly—he was used to answering this question every few months. 'Leave us alone.'

The constable didn't look convinced. 'I haven't spoken to him in the last ten years,' Shaikh reiterated, straightening the creases of his white kurta–pyjama. Distressed by the impatient knocks on the door, he hadn't had the time to wear his skullcap, which now lay forgotten by his bedside.

Shaikh's son is believed to be in the United Kingdom, in the city of Birmingham. Shaikh had decided to send Rahil's wife and children to Rahil, after being detained for a week during the crackdown following the attacks. With two of his sons already behind bars, he understood the risk in Rahil's return.

But the money trail leading to his other son Faisal is also baffling. Why was so much black money being circulated? Was it only for the house in Bandra and the luxury he lived in? If so, what had Faisal done to receive so much money? Why did a few of these men, all Sunnis, go for Ziyarat to Iran?

In his confessional statement, Tanveer had said that he had taken training in jihad to avenge the atrocities committed against Muslims in Kashmir, Palestine, Chechnya and some parts of Iraq. So were they training for the 7/11 blasts or were they sleeper cells on their way to fight abroad?

Is Yug Mohit Chaudhry right? Did the investigating agencies catch only the small fry because they were unable to trace the real masterminds behind the blasts? Could a few of those convicted actually be innocent or merely have been involved on the periphery?

It is a fact that investigating agencies were unsuccessful in naming a single person from Pakistan's ISI or prosecuting any of the LeT masterminds in India. Arif Qasmani, a financier for the LeT and later the Al-Qaeda, had met Faisal in Pakistan. But he wasn't cited as an absconder, as the ATS was unable to establish any links between him and the money being circulated in India. Qasmani's role came to the fore only after a US Department of Treasury's release that stated that he had supported the LeT in executing the blasts.

A second name figured in Faisal's confession—Abdul Razzak. He was the man who introduced Faisal to Qasmani and was later said to have come to Mumbai to help execute the attacks. But the uncanny similarities between Abdul Razzak and Abdul Razzak Masood, an accused in the Sai Baba temple blasts case, have perplexed many of those who analysed the case.

Abdul Razzak Masood was a commerce graduate from Delhi. In 2005, he was detained in Iran for five months after the Indian government blacklisted him for his connections with the LeT. He was deported to India and arrested in August 2005, charged with being an LeT coordinator for Dubai. After being interrogated for over a year by both Indian and international agencies, he spent another two years in jail before he was granted bail in 2009. In October 2012, he hanged himself at his Hyderabad residence. He was working as a roadside vendor at the time.

The ATS could never find the Abdul Razzak named in the 7/11 blasts charge sheet. But the similarities between Razzak and Masood are startling. Both were said to have been born in Hyderabad and involved in recruiting Indians for the LeT. As per records, the Abdul Razzak from the 7/11 train blasts case met Faisal's brother Rahil in 2003 in Dubai. At the time, Masood too was said to be an LeT coordinator in the same city.

This begs the question: could they be the same person?

As of today, SIMI is the only Indian terror group convicted of being involved in the blasts. The IM claimed responsibility for the attack several times over the course of the 7/11 case trial. But these claims were never substantially investigated by any other agency, perhaps because it could have poked holes in the rest of the 7/11 investigation. In sharp contrast to this, when two outfits—one Muslim, one Hindu—were suspected in the Samjhauta train blasts of 2007, both the CBI and NIA joined forces to look into the allegations. Was there lack of political will to conduct a similarly thorough investigation into the 7/11 blasts?

There are two other terror cases related to the 7/11 blasts: the Aurangabad arms haul and the Malegaon terror strike. The blame for both cases too was affixed on some of the people arrested in the 7/11 case. Faisal was named an accused (and was later convicted) in the Aurangabad arms haul case, whereas Asif's and Mohammed Ali's names figured in the Malegaon blasts case. The brother of one of the accused in the Malegaon case was also tried and convicted in the Aurangabad arms haul case.

Which begs another question: are these three cases really linked to one another? But then, weren't the blasts in Malegaon, a city with an 86 per cent Muslim population, later alleged to be a revenge attack by Hindu extremists? Was arresting a similar set of accused in all the three cases a mistake and did little more than weaken ATS's own investigation in each case? Why could they not acknowledge the possibility of Hindu extremism before Swami Aseemanand, the prime accused in the Samjhauta blasts case, spilt the beans a few weeks after he was charged?

The Islamist group SIMI was branded a terrorist organization and banned in 2001. However, Abhinav Bharat, the group of Hindu extremists alleged to have taken part in the Samjhauta train blasts and the 2008 Malegaon blasts, is yet to face similar censure.

Nevertheless, one thing is clear. There needs to be a complete overhaul of how investigating agencies perceive and investigate cases related to terrorism, and it should go beyond religion. Agencies should steer clear of making tall claims at the outset when their investigation is unscientific. Doing this is only an affront to every victim of terror—living, injured or dead.

That day, the constable left Atta-ur Rahman Shaikh's residence with a warning: 'Get in touch with us when you find out more.' If only the premier investigating agencies of the country showed such tenacity.

Note on the Sources

The 7/11 serial train blasts, and the case that followed, has been shrouded in controversy from the very beginning. The legal complexities required us to look at a series of events—including what happened in the years that would follow—as a whole so that we could paint a complete picture.

We have accessed several documents with regard to the case, which are a part of the book. Records and proceedings of the 7/11 blasts case include remand applications, the roznama of the case to understand the progression of the trial—which ran into hundreds of pages—the charge sheet, the statements of witnesses from both the prosecution and the defence, the affidavits filed by the injured victims, the several orders on applications and the petitions filed in the special MCOCA court, the Bombay High Court and the Supreme Court, and the 1839-page judgement.

However, reporting on the train blasts case was more difficult than one could ever imagine because of the restrictions placed on the media. For instance, at one point in time during the case, the media was banned from reporting on the investigation into the possible role of the Indian Mujahideen in the blasts. This was after Sadiq Israr Shaikh from the IM was taken into custody by the Anti-Terrorism Squad.

The blasts happened when one of us was a trainee reporter and the other was still in school. To fill the gaps, we used articles published in several other media organizations, mainly *The Times of India*, *Mumbai Mirror*, *The Indian Express*, *Midday* and the online portal Rediff.com. Interviews of officials involved in the investigation of the blasts and their statements in court were useful in presenting how the police took the case forward.

One of the authors was present in court during most proceedings, especially during Advocate Yug Mohit Chaudhry and Special Public Prosecutor Raja Thakre's final arguments, as well the day the sentence was read out. The other one was present during Sadiq Israr Shaikh's deposition.

With regard to the 2001 SIMI ban, we accessed the ban notification and several witness statements.

Most details about Faisal Atta-ur Rahman Shaikh in the chapter 'The Good Life' have been taken from his confession, prime witness accounts and during our interactions with him, his father and the co-accused in the case. We also gathered information from the investigators who interrogated him. Our meetings with the accused in the court corridors during the course of the trial proved very helpful in observing their mannerisms and understanding their point of view.

Our interactions with their families proved most helpful. The men and their kin have always maintained that they are innocent.

The chapter on Vinod Bhatt, 'The Suicide Mystery', has been written after speaking to his colleagues who did not wish to be named and Ehtesham Siddiqui's testimony in court.

With regard to the chapters 'The Good Life', 'Maximum Damage' and 'Preparation and Execution', we took certain situational liberties to explain the series of events as the investigators saw it—for instance, narrative liberties have been taken by us while describing the time Faisal and his friends went to a club. We wove the narrative based on his confession, the way he behaved in court and our meetings with the accused. We would like to specify that these are not comments made by the authors; these are the sequence of events accepted by the court.

Details about the meetings in 2006 have been written on the basis of the confessional statements of the accused and the testimony of Faisal's friend Mohammad Alam Qureshi. We realized there were several contradictions about the events in the confessional statements and in these circumstances, we relied on the version the prosecution used in the case.

There are a few things we noticed while writing this book. While the confessional statements had a lot of detail about the accused, especially their backgrounds, the details regarding the planning and execution of the blasts were comparatively sketchy.

For the chapters 'Terror Revisits' and 'A Bomb for a Bomb', we have relied on our interviews with investigators and victims, and *Tehelka* reporter Ashish Khetan's expose on Aseemanand's confession. Despite having a copy of the original confession, we have chosen to run it under *Tehelka*'s name as they were the first ones to break the news.

'The Terror Trail', 'Breakthrough', 'The Pakistani Mercenary—An Encounter' and 'A Soldier from Pakistan' rely mainly on investigator accounts and the defence in court during these episodes. We have also used documents wherever possible.

In the chapter titled 'The Courtroom Cast', all the information on Shahid Azmi has been sourced from Kalid Azmi, Shahid's brother, interviews with several defence lawyers, news stories, courtroom staff and journalists. An interview published in Rediff.com on 28 July 2007 was especially helpful. All of Shahid's thoughts in the chapter have been narrated aloud to the people interviewed by us. Nikhil Dixit's piece 'Shahid Azmi never tried to hide his past as Tada detainee' was of great help while writing this chapter.

Everything that happened in Special Judge Mridula Bhatkar's courtroom has been well-documented and the nitty-gritty details were sourced from the people present in court at that time. The incident involving the then jail superintendent, Swati Sathe, appears in the petitions filed in the High Court and Supreme Court. Interviews of prisoners who witnessed the accused being beaten up after the alarm bell went off helped us understand the details of the incident better.

The chapter on Shahid Azmi's murder is based on our interactions with his family and the officers privy to the details of his murder.

We have gone through all the documents that connect Sadiq Israr Shaikh with the blasts in the chapter '"We did it"—Indian Mujahideen', which include his statement under section 164 to the magistrate, who witnessed his testimony. We also accessed his 'confession' that first appeared on CNN-IBN in February 2009. The events that preceded his arrest have been sourced from officers (court as well as investigative) who do not wish to be named. *Mumbai Mirror*'s article on the famous press conference from 2008 proved to be a wealth of information for us.

We have also read David Coleman Headley's NIA interrogation report to understand the structure of the LeT and books like *Black Friday* by S. Hussain Zaidi, *The Siege* by Adrian Levy and Cathy Scott Clark, and *Indian Mujahideen* by Shishir Gupta. We have also referred to several articles written by Praveen Swami, currently working with *The Indian Express*, to understand more about these terror outfits.

The chapter based on the trial, 'A Witness, a Confession and a Pressure Cooker', has been sourced from several documents, interviews with all the lawyers involved in the case and the accused. There are a lot of people, including police officers and former SIMI activists, who spoke to us on the condition of anonymity. For 'Volte-face', we were present in court as the drama unfolded.

During the course of our research, we also came across several incidents that were not and could not be documented. We have tried to rely mainly on those events that could be substantiated in some way or the other.

All the victims mentioned in the last chapter have been interviewed by us.

Acknowledgements

Generally, in cases of terror, the society presumes the accused is guilty—before the man even stands trial. This book attempts to present both sides of the story surrounding the 7/11 train blasts case.

There are two cardinal principles of journalism: to question thoroughly and to represent fairly. We have based our book on these two principles, while attempting to unfold all the layers of this complex crime. However, this voyage would have been incomplete without contributions from a lot of people.

We would first like to thank the families of each of the victims, who recounted the most horrific days of their lives and the struggles they had to go through. The pain their families went through was immeasurable, and so many of them are still stuck in that pain.

We have met a few of the hundreds of investigators connected to the case, who helped us understand the constraints they were working under, with pressure from the media and the government increasing every passing day. They also divulged several interesting with details, but many of those cannot be placed on record. We would specifically like to thank Assistant Commissioner of Police P.B. Rathod, ACP Vasant

Tajne (retired) and ACP Iqbal Shaikh (retired) for fielding the volley of questions from us for hours.

Lawyers—both from the prosecution as well as the defence—have been a gold mine of information. Supporting all their claims with legal documents, they patiently cooperated with us, helping us understand the complexities of the case— not only for the book but also during the course of the trial, while we were reporting on the case. Notable among them are advocates Sharif Shaikh, defence counsel Yug Mohit Chaudhry, Special Public Prosecutor Raja Thakare, defence lawyers Prakash Shetty and Wahab Khan.

We interviewed several SIMI activists in the by-lanes of Kurla, where the concept of cafes does not exist. They parted with a lot of valuable information about things happening on ground zero—all this, while being thrown out of one Udipi restaurant or another (as interviews aren't allowed in these places). We would also like to thank Gulzar Azmi, the secretary (legal cell) of the Jamiat-Ulama-e-Maharashtra, and Shahid Ansari, who handles their media cell.

Abdul Wahid Shaikh, the only accused in the case to be acquitted, spent several hours with us, helping us in every way possible and parting with all the information he could. We are especially grateful to him. New Delhi–based lawyer Ashok Agarwal also helped us with several documents regarding the ban on SIMI.

Apart from government officials, if there is one person who recreated 11 July 2006 for us, it would be journalist Paresh Mishra, who runs a news agency called News Stock Monitoring Services Pvt. Ltd. Since he found himself in the midst of this disaster, he began helping with rescue operations till late into the night, the disaster unfolding right before his eyes.

Senior crime journalist Mateen Hafeez, assistant editor with *The Times of India*, who has reported extensively on the investigations into the case, was very helpful. Several of his news articles have been referred to in the book.

We are grateful to photographers Deepak Salvi from Live Photo, and Prashant Narvekar and Tariq Khan, who willingly contributed their work for the book.

Juggling the writing of the book with our daily work was far from easy, so here is a big thank you to our peers, especially senior correspondent from *Hindustan Times* Charul Shah.

Friends like Alka Shukla, Omkar Khandekar, Pallabi Munsi and IPS officer Quaiser Khalid helped us out in whatever way they could.

We must thank our editor-in-chief at *Mumbai Mirror*, Meenal Baghel, for believing in us always. Ms Baghel has encouraged our zeal, making us delve deeper into the intricacies of terror reporting.

We would also like to especially thank Milee Ashwarya and Jyotsna Raman, our editors at Penguin Random House India, for accommodating every missed deadline. We would also like to thank Kavitha Iyer, who works as an associate editor with *The Indian Express*, for editing and adding value to a few chapters on an extremely tight deadline.

A person may have numerous ideas, but without an opportunity, there is little that one can do. We are grateful to S. Hussain Zaidi for giving us the platform to work on a subject we are extremely passionate about. He believed in us and reinforced our confidence as we worked on the book. Mr Zaidi did not just edit our chapters, he also taught us the fine art of storytelling.

A special thanks to our colleague at *Mumbai Mirror*, special correspondent Jyoti Shelar. She was our go-to person in times of crisis and has helped us put this book together. Her gift of listening patiently to our rambling cleared the mental clutter for us.

Right at the fag end of the book, Shreya Shah, a thorough journalist, gave us her invaluable inputs, pointed out anomalies and tied up loose ends. Thank you, Shreya, for doing much more than what we could have imagined.

For the legal aspects, we had full faith in Sunil Baghel, senior assistant editor with *Mumbai Mirror*. Thanks, Sunil, for your unending support and contribution till the very end.

It would be very remiss of us if we did not thank our families for the unquestioning support they extended to us as we wrote this book. Thank you, Fatema Matiwala, parents, Shabbir and Shaheen Indorewala, and siblings, Sameer and Mojh Indorewala.